A history
of the principles of
librarianship

By the same author:

Books: an anthology (1968)
English studies: a guide for librarians (1971)
An introduction to university library administration (2nd ed, 1974)
Library power (1974)

A history
of the principles of
librarianship

by

JAMES THOMPSON
Librarian, University of Reading

CLIVE BINGLEY
LONDON

LINNET BOOKS
HAMDEN · CONN

*To my wife Mary, my daughter
Rosalind and my son Gabriel*

FIRST PUBLISHED 1977 BY CLIVE BINGLEY LTD
16 PEMBRIDGE ROAD LONDON W11
SIMULTANEOUSLY PUBLISHED IN THE USA BY LINNET BOOKS
AN IMPRINT OF THE SHOE STRING PRESS INC
995 SHERMAN AVENUE HAMDEN CONNECTICUT 06514
SET IN 12 ON 13 POINT ALDINE ROMAN BY ALLSET
AND PRINTED IN THE UK BY REDWOOD BURN LTD
OF TROWBRIDGE AND ESHER
COPYRIGHT © JAMES THOMPSON 1977
ALL RIGHTS RESERVED
BINGLEY ISBN: 0-85157-241-3
LINNET ISBN: 0-208-01661-9

Library of Congress Cataloging in Publication Data

Thompson, James.
    A history of the principles of librarianship.

    Bibliography: p.
    Includes index.
      1. Library science—History. 2. Libraries—History.
I. Title.
Z665.T497   020'.9   77-3335
ISBN 0-208-01661-9

Contents

Preface

I had intended to strike an original note by declaring that this venture into library history was not motivated by any interest in the antiquarian or the curious. I have discovered, however, that without exception my many predecessors in the field have lodged similar disclaimers. John Willis Clark, for example, registered the hope that *The care of books*, his essay on the history of libraries and their fittings, would serve 'to impart human interest' to the subject. Raymond Irwin, in his turn, aimed with *The origins of the English library* to set the history of libraries 'in perspective against the development of our civilization'. And, to conclude with a more recent example, Thomas Kelly introduces his history of public libraries in Great Britain with the following quotation from Pierce Butler: 'Librarianship, as we know it, can be fully apprehended only through an understanding of its historic origins'.

My own purpose is very straightforward. I seek to establish the historical foundations for a current theory of librarianship. This therefore makes the present work something of a companion to my *Library power*, published in 1974. *Library power* was an attempt to promote a philosophy of librarianship which, though new, was based on some well-proved principles. I felt at the time that a longer and more detailed examination of the historical development of the major principles of librarianship would be a worthwhile contribution to professional literature. Hence the present work.

The structure of the book is simple. The first chapter is general and introductory, and the subsequent chapters each deal with a particular aspect of librarianship in a separate but not necessarily self-contained way. Though references are grouped after each chapter, I have nevertheless also included at the end of the book a summary bibliography of those works from which substantial help was obtained.

CHAPTER ONE
First principles

There have been libraries in the world for more than twenty-five centuries. The great Alexandrian Library was already flourishing two hundred years before the birth of Christ, and it is unlikely that the advanced and clearcut principles on which it was conceived and organised sprang forth full-formed without precedents of any kind. Long before even the Alexandrian Library, in Nineveh in the reign of Ashur-banipal (668-626 BC), there existed a library of some tens of thousands of clay tablets which was as comprehensive and as well-arranged as any equivalent national library of modern times.

So long is the time span covered by the existence of libraries that it must follow that the main principles of librarianship are by now exceptionally well-established. Only the most ignorant individual would, in professional terms, set out to re-invent the wheel. Conversely, it also follows that the decisions of any librarian, even in apparently the most contemporary of situations, will always benefit from a return to first principles. It is after all a fact that we base our lives on previous experience, and can predict our future only on the basis of past performance. As H M Cashmore wrote some years ago: (1) 'All good workers appreciate that they stand on the shoulders of others. They are grateful for what their more primitive predecessors have done and perform their own tasks more intelligently and efficiently if they have studied the stages in the development of their art.'

Cashmore's remarks were made in the context of the history of library cataloguing. Berwick Sayers (2) made precisely the same point in relation to the history of library classification schemes, stressing 'the obvious need for the reasonably equipped librarian to know the history of the instruments which he uses every day'. And Lawrence S Thompson (3) goes so far as to consider library history as 'an invaluable aid to future generations in their attempt to avoid the errors of the past'.

While it remains true that librarians must build on the experience of their own past, it is unfortunately equally true that the development of libraries and librarianship has not been some kind of evolutionary process whereby these have grown better and better. Some 'primitive predecessors' were very much more effective in what they did than many of their successors; and it is not only from 'the errors of the past' that a librarian can learn, but from the neglected and unacknowledged triumphs also. It appears as often as not that our predecessors, in their own terms, knew the true path: a viewpoint expressed very fairly and accurately by DM Norris (4) in her book on the history of cataloguing and cataloguing methods: 'The term, History, suggests rather an evolutionary, or gradual development, but such is not the case with cataloguing; the ancients were as proficient in the art as we are to-day, but their methods were different. So it is throughout the ages, and therefore this is not a history, but a survey of the methods used for compiling lists of books.'

An even more perceptive view has been offered by E A Savage. (5) Savage propounds a theory of 'occultations', observing that since the technology of librarianship is limited and narrow, 'An enthusiastic librarian diligently searches for new ideas, but rarely discovers any. The open shelf is the oldest of ideas. Book classification is a medieval, probably a very ancient method. The classed catalogue, about which we wrangled with fishwives' pertinacity thirty or forty years ago, existed in the fifteenth century, and Bodley and his librarian James contended about subject cataloguing, as vigorously as we have done, but more politely, in early Jacobean times. James, by the way, was as obstinate in his insistence upon the value of subject cataloguing as any modern librarian could be. He compiled such a catalogue—and a good one—of part of the Bodleian, and his manuscript may be seen in Oxford to-day by anybody who is interested. At one time reading lists and co-operative cataloguing seemed to me new, until I discovered that the Grey Friars used both methods in the thirteenth century. And bookbinding: what progress has that made? Notes about binding are unusual in monastic library catalogues, but the catalogue of the Leicester Abbey Library describes methods that we employ to-day for some of the books we wish to preserve most carefully. The truth is that the chief processes in library administration undergo periodical occultations. They emerge again the brighter for their eclipse, and shine upon us for a time, and fade again into obscurity. We lose ideas, regain them, fight against them, yield to them, and forget them once more.'

The following chapters of this present work in effect trace the waxings and wanings of at least the major ideas which have characterised librarianship; and it is a remarkable fact that despite both current and former 'occultations', the essential principles of librarianship emerge unambiguously and incontrovertibly from our long history. Good ideas are seen to be good ideas on the basis of factual, almost statistical, evidence. Bad ideas are equally and similarly identifiable. As Arthur E Bostwick (6) observed in his history of the American public library, though scarcely a line of library development 'has not been followed too far or given one or another odd twist by some one', nevertheless overall 'the growth has been healthy and has followed directions of proved advantage'.

The foregoing remarks would seem to point to the possibility of establishing a coherent and well-attested philosophy of librarianship, and the reader must judge the validity of this hypothesis by examining the proofs offered in subsequent chapters. Previous writers have not been so confident, but they have nevertheless been aware of the possibility. DMNorris,

11

cited earlier as declaring her work on cataloguing to be, not a history, but a non-evolutionary uncritical survey, nevertheless concludes her study with an unequivocal and practical statement of the main principles which govern the making of library catalogues. Savage also, one can infer, realises that if methods and techniques of librarianship which were found satisfactory in early times have re-appeared and been found equally satisfactory in our own times, then some identifiably satisfactory principles must exist.

Other writers, however, though accepting that a degree of coherence is now detectable in the principles which govern librarianship, then fall into the error of believing that this coherence has existed for only the last hundred years or so. In Predeek's history of libraries in Great Britain and North America, (7) it is maintained that British librarianship started 'only with the founding of the Library Association and the public library movement': thereby, in one phrase, dismissing the possibility that, for example, medieval libraries in this country may have made any permanent or substantial contribution to the principles of librarianship. In Predeek's history also, it is claimed that in the United States 'librarianship as a coherent phenomenon is young': whereas in truth, librarianship in that country is no younger than the country itself, and many of its principles (as opposed to its achievements) go right back to colonial days.

The difficulty perhaps rests in the fact that though librarianship itself is not young, the examination and interpretation of the history of libraries is. The pioneer here, as in so many other matters, acknowledged and unacknowledged, was Edward Edwards. His monumental two-volume *Memoirs of libraries*—not published, after all, until 1859 —was the first major attempt of this kind. What Edwards really wanted to do was to write a revealing and interpretative 'biography' of a library: to bring, in his own words, 'an untired reader face to face with the founders and patrons, the organisers and the students, who, generation after generation, busied themselves in building up one of the great Libraries of the world'. He felt able, however, only to pursue a humbler aim, namely to 'bring together materials which have hitherto been widely scattered, and arrange them, to the best of my ability, in serviceable order', but he was confident nevertheless that the resultant work would aid 'even in its narrative portions, certain measures for the extension and increased efficiency of British Libraries, belonging to the public—measures which seem to me to possess practical and immediate importance'.

Edwards was a great believer in providing statistical and historical evidence in support of whatever argument he was presenting. The major campaign of his life was to promote the establishment of free municipal libraries throughout Britain, and he underpinned this campaign with publications such as his *Remarks on the paucity of libraries freely open to the public, in the British Empire; together with a succinct statistical view of the existing provision of Public Libraries in the several states of Europe* (1848), which took the form of a letter addressed to the Earl of Ellesmere, the Chairman of the Royal Commission then enquiring into the management and affairs of the British Museum, using materials he had collected for an article in the *British quarterly review* and a paper he had delivered to the Statistical Society.

He set about his *Memoirs of libraries* in the same way. It is in two parts. The first five hundred or so pages deal with the history of libraries, from those of the ancient world, then of the Middle Ages, and all the way down to the 'Parisian Bibliothèque *Imperiale*' of his own day: an exhausting and exhaustive mass of information. The second part of his book, again some five hundred or so pages, deals with what he calls the 'economy of libraries'—the creation of book collections, the design of buildings, classification and cataloguing, library administration and service to the public. It obviously seemed only logical to Edwards that he should preface a practical exposition of the principles of librarianship by an historical account of libraries. He defends this approach first by remarking severely that 'to foster no reverence for the generations which are gone, is a sure sign that men have nothing within', and secondly by declaring that 'the narrative that shall worthily tell of the growth of great Libraries will be none the less truly historical for the care that may be taken to link with the story its true bearings on the present management, the assured permanence, and the liberal extension, of those mind-armouries with which it has to deal'.

Edwards was profoundly aware of the value of *Memoirs of libraries*. Even at the end of his days, in poverty and neglect, he still sought to bring out a further edition of this his major work, which in his own words had been 'the chief delight of some of the best years of my life'. But in fact the book never sold well, and to the majority of modern librarians it is no more than a familiar but unread title.

Another defect in any theory that librarianship as a coherent body of principles is a relatively recent phenomenon is that such a view is contradicted by the recorded witness of individual voices right down the ages. A straightforward illustration of this can be obtained by considering the provenance of the clearest of modern principles of librarianship: namely, that libraries are for all.

It is no surprise to read that Archibald MacLeish, the Librarian of Congress from 1939 to 1944, defined that Library's three categories of user as follows: 'first, the members of Congress; second, officers of the Federal Government and the staffs of various government departments and agencies including the Supreme Court and its Bar; and, third, the general public—all comers from all places'. (8) This mid-twentieth century definition was a necessary clarification on the part of MacLeish, following the long incumbencies of his two giant predecessors in the same office—Ainsworth Rand Spofford and Herbert Putnam—but his 'all comers from all places' was by that time no revolutionary call.

However, it is more surprising to read this identical principle, even more vehemently expressed, in the evidence which Antonio Panizzi gave in London in 1836, before the Select Committee on the British Museum: 'I want a poor student to have the same means of indulging his learned curiosity, of

14

following his rational pursuits, of consulting the same authorities, of fathoming the most intricate enquiry as the richest
man in the kingdom, as far as books go, and I contend that
the Government is bound to give him the most liberal and unlimited assistance in this respect'. (9) Panizzi was here promoting a principle which was not then as socially acceptable
as in MacLeish's time, but between him and MacLeish as librarians the hundred year gap does not exist at all.

But two hundred years before even Panizzi, early in the
seventeenth century, Gabriel Naudé—librarian to Cardinal
Mazarin and author of what is regarded as the first important
treatise on library science, *Avis pour dresser une bibliothèque*
(1627)—had declared of the great library of which he had
charge: 'It shall be open to all the world, without excluding a
living soul . . . . From its door shall resound that cry which
never yet been heard in the Republic of Letters: "Come in,
all you who desire to read, come in freely".' (10) Naudé was
wrong only in one respect: the cry had been heard before, as
far back as ancient times. But again the existence of this
basic principle of librarianship can be seen as being no modern
phenomenon.

It seems strange to have to argue that librarianship has solid
foundations, and that its principles have by and large been
established over a very long period of time, especially since
such a view is very readily accepted of most other subjects
and disciplines. With regard to chemistry, for example, whilst
the great volume and high importance of contemporary work
is acknowledged, even the layman realises that modern chem-
ists are unlikely to dismiss out of hand the contributions made
by such illustrious predecessors as Robert Boyle in the
seventeenth century, Joseph Priestley and Antoine Lavoisier
in the eighteenth, and Humphrey Davy in the early nineteenth
century. It behoves librarians to respect their past also, and
not to fall too readily under the sway of every trend and
fashion of the day at the expense of first principles.

The approach of the present work is to examine in turn
the genesis of various aspects of librarianship, starting with

15

the growth of library collections, whether of clay tablets, manuscripts, or books; continuing with the preservation and conservation of those materials; and then dealing with the regulation of access to them. Subsequent chapters look at the purposes of libraries, the role of the librarian, library cataloguing and classification, and finally, the physical design of libraries. At the end of the book an attempt will be made to summarise the main principles of librarianship which reveal themselves as a result of this examination.

References

1 Foreword to NORRIS, D M: *A history of cataloguing*, 1939.

2 SAYERS, W C Berwick: *An introduction to library classification*, 9th ed, 1955.

3 Preface to PREDEEK, A: *A history of libraries in Great Britain and North America*, 1947.

4 NORRIS, D M, *op cit*, 1.

5 Introduction to THORNTON, J L: *The chronology of librarianship*, 1941.

6 BOSTWICK, A E: *The American public library*, 1910.

7 PREDEEK, A, *op cit*, 3.

8 Quoted in GOODRUM, C A: *The Library of Congress*, 1974.

9 Quoted in MILLER, E: *Prince of librarians*, 1967.

10 Quoted in EDWARDS, E: *Memoirs of libraries*, 1859.

CHAPTER TWO

The size of library collections

1 THE FIRST GREAT LIBRARIES

One of the earliest recorded statements of library policy is that relating to the greatest library of antiquity, the Alexandrian Library. The historian Josephus (1) reports that 'Demetrios of Phaleron, who was in charge of the king's library, was anxious to collect, if he could, all the books in the inhabited world, and, if he heard of, or saw, any book worthy of study, he would buy it'.

Alexandria itself was founded by Alexander the Great early in 331 BC, on his way down the Nile from Memphis, on the western extremity of the delta, west of the Canopic branch of the river and between Lake Mareotis and the sea. Alexander was personally responsible for the plan of the main part of the city, though he stayed there only briefly. It was characteristic of Alexander to seek to diffuse the language and civilisation of Greece wherever victory led him, and indeed he went on to establish Greek cities throughout Asia.

Early in the Ptolemaic period Alexandria became the capital of Egypt, and by the middle of the third century BC was the most magnificent city in the Mediterranean area. Ptolemy Soter, a general of Alexander's who eventually came to rule Egypt (323-285) and was the founder of the Ptolemaic dynasty, set out to develop Alexandria as a cultural centre. It was he who founded the famous Library, between 300 and 290 BC. As recounted by Edward Alexander Parsons, (2)

17

Soter created an empire that lasted three centuries, built a city that was a wonder of the earth for seven hundred years, and made the Museum-Library an intellectual beacon for nine hundred years.

The Greeks of Alexandria came from the most varied parts of the Greek world, and possessed 'complex traditions of religion, mythology, and poetry'. (3)

Under Soter and his successors (Ptolemy Philadelphus and Ptolemy Euergetes), there gathered a large group of scholars and intelligentsia, attracted by the prospect of 'an affluent, carefree, and peaceful life', (4) inhabiting the Museum and having available to them the great resources of the Library. This kind of patronage by a king was a very ancient feature of Greek culture, and there were even 'clear indications in the second century that the Ptolemies were prepared to forestall, by force if necessary, the defection of a scholar to a rival camp, particularly that of Pergamon'. (5)

The same degree of ruthlessness was apparent in the efforts of the Ptolemies to create the biggest and most important library in the world. Soter's adviser, Demetrios of Phaleron, collected in less than ten or twelve years some 200,000 papyrus rolls. Ptolemy Philadelphus and his successor Ptolemy Euergetes, as Edward Edwards relates, (6) caused all books imported into Egypt by foreigners to be seized, transcribed, the copies delivered to the owners, and the originals deposited in the Library; Euergetes borrowed the works of Sophocles, Euripides and Aeschylus from the Athenians, and though he conducted the whole business in exactly the same way, he did at least make a payment of fifteen talents (the equivalent, in Edwards's time, of some £3,000) for the exchange. Then again, when Eumenes II (197-159 BC) strove to match his library at Pergamon (which according to Plutarch eventually amounted to 200,000 items) with that at Alexandria, 'The Egyptians are supposed to have cut off the supply of papyrus being sent to Pergamon to prevent its library from growing as large as that in Alexandria. The librarians at Pergamon then developed a new writing material, parchment (from the

Latin *Pergamene*), as a substitute for papyrus.' (7) In a rather more constructive way, the scholars, librarians and bibliographers of the Alexandria Library actually produced books: preparing editions of, and commentaries on, classical authors; and organising translations, such as the very large undertaking, involving a great number of scholars, under Demetrios—the translation of the Scriptures from Hebrew into Greek.

The outcome of this approach was that eventually the Alexandrian Library must have contained most of the extant literature of the period. It is difficult to compute the size of the Library in modern terms, because a 'book' then was a roll of papyrus. A roll of papyrus, which was not normally longer than thirty-five feet, could contain not more than two or three books of Homer, or a single Greek play; an author's collected works, therefore, would usually take up a number of rolls. In Edwards's words, (8) 'the rolls of the ancients might be regarded as only parts of books'; but even so, he and most other library historians have reckoned that the Alexandrian Library contained the equivalent of 700,000 volumes. The only notable writer to have doubted this was William Blades, who commented: (9) 'Before the invention of Printing, books were comparatively scarce; and, knowing as we do, how very difficult it is, even after the steam-press has been working for half a century, to make a collection of half a million books, we are forced to receive with great incredulity the accounts in old writers of the wonderful extent of ancient libraries'. Blades does not believe that there were anything like 700,000, or even 500,000 volumes, in the Alexandrian Library. But though his cautionary note as to the number of items should be heeded, no authority has ever contested that the Alexandrian Library was not the greatest Library of antiquity and the greatest before the invention of printing; and certainly one writer, Parsons, (10) has claimed with justifiable conviction that it was 'perhaps potentially the most important ever collected'.

To return now to the statement of library policy by Demetrios, with which this chapter began. The aspirations of the

Alexandrian Library were a direct reflection of the aspirations of Alexandria itself: to be a focus of all Hellenic learning and culture. The Alexandrian Library was therefore a national library of Greek literature. Its primary aim and its guiding principle was to bring together the 'complete corpus of Greek literature'. (11)

In addition, there are grounds for suggesting that works in other languages were represented in translation: the Hebrew Bible, for example; ancient Egyptian texts; and it is possible that works of Latin literature were acquired before the end of the Ptolemaic period. In sum, the principle was established that a national library should contain all national literature, along with some representation of other national literatures.

Though there were of course other libraries in ancient times, they are dominated historically by two libraries in particular: one, the Alexandrian Library, has been surveyed. The other was the great clay tablet library of Ashurbanipal, king of Assyria 668-626 BC. Indeed, Parsons notes that Assyrian enthusiasts believe that this library was the forerunner of the Alexandrian Library, even to the extent of considering that Callimachus—the Alexandrian Library's great cataloguer—followed the 'technical library rules' found in the library of Ashurbanipal.

Ashurbanipal was the last of the great Sargonids: Sargon (722-705 BC) was succeeded by his son Sennacherib (705-681), his grandson Esarhaddon (681-669), and then by Ashurbanipal who moved the royal capital to Nineveh, which city then became the centre of Assyrian civilisation and the administrative centre of a kingdom which stretched from the Persian Gulf to the Mediterranean.

Ashurbanipal prided himself on his learning, and as a patron of the arts. He sent agents to every part of his empire and to foreign lands also, to collect 'written records of all kinds and on all subjects', (12) and accumulated a library of some 30,000 clay tablets at Nineveh. These clay tablets were a few inches square, and characters were inscribed on them with a sharp implement while the clay was still soft. It says much for their durability that the great Assyriologist, Sir Henry Layard (1817-1894) found vast quantities of them still extant during his excavations at Nineveh in the mid-nineteenth century, and some 20,000 are now in the British Museum. Ashurbanipal employed a very large number of scribes and scholars in the work of compiling and editing the thousands of texts so brought together.

Ashurbanipal's library contained religious texts, prayers, incantations, rituals and charms; materials on history, government, geography, law, legends and mythology, astronomy and astrology, biology, mathematics, medicine and natural history; and in addition a collection of what can be described as official publications—copies of letters to and from ambassadors, for example, and tax lists. As well as Assyrian works, there were copies and translations from other nations, including predecessors (represented by translations of Sumerian and Babylonian texts).

The library at Nineveh, therefore, while pre-dating the Alexandrian Library by some centuries, nevertheless plainly also subscribed to the principle of national completeness, while equally not neglecting the representation in translation of other national literatures. This principle did not re-appear —indeed, did not need to re-appear because there were no subsequent libraries on such a scale until modern times—for two thousand years, until the emergence of the British Museum Library and the Library of Congress. The successors of Ptolemy Soter and Ashurbanipal, in library terms, were Antonio Panizzi and Ainsworth Rand Spofford.

2 THE LIBRARIES OF THE MIDDLE AGES

In the chronology of libraries and librarianship, the next significant period was the Middle Ages. If the library at Nineveh was the age of the clay tablet, and the Alexandrian Library the age of the papyrus roll, then medaeval libraries represent the age of the manuscript—writings on parchment, in codex form.

The fall of the Roman Empire and the rise to power of the barbarian tribes were not conducive to the growth of libraries. As Elmer D Johnson has poignantly expressed it, (13) 'With the destruction of ancient centers of learning, the great libraries of antiquity were gone forever. For nearly a thousand years the typical European library was to be the small collection of manuscripts laboriously copied and jealously guarded, in the many monasteries scattered from Greece to Iceland. Instead of the magnificent temple library, with its thousands of rolls in vaulted marble rooms, the library of the Middle Ages was more often a collection of a few hundred codices kept in a bookchest or two in the corner of a monastery chapel.' Thus the common word for library in the early Middle Ages was *armarium*, the name for the bookchest where the books were kept; and the librarian of such a collection was known as the *armarius*.

Sir Frederic Kenyon (14) notes that the earliest monastic Rule (the code of discipline observed by a religious order)— that of St Pachomius in Egypt in the first half of the fourth century—provides for the storing of books in a cupboard, and their loan under careful conditions to the brethren. The books so issued were substantial treatises, such as Augustine's Homilies on St John, the Pastoral Rule of St Gregory, the works of Hugo de St Victor, the Synonyms of Isidore, and Jerome on the Prophets. The Benedictine Rule, which recommended that each brother should have a book to read, presupposed that each monastery library would contain 'enough books for each brother to be able to borrow one'. (15) Johnson points out that once this ratio was achieved, the growth of the collection was slow; and he provides a few statistics—St Gall had 400 volumes in 841; Cluny, 570 in the twelfth century, and Bobbio, about the same time, had 650; St Pons de Tomières in France, as late as the thirteenth century, had only 300. He points out, though, that the average volume was large, and often contained two or more works; and that a good number were *florilegia*, or selections from many authors, giving 'a wide sampling of literature in a relatively small space'.

Even the history of libraries in the Middle Ages is, however, essentially the history of growth and multiplication, slow though it was. Towards the twelfth century, the monastic library gave way in importance to the cathedral library, which was, in Johnson's words, 'designed for educational rather than inspirational reading'. Again Johnson provides a few statistics: the cathedral library at Durham had some 600 volumes in the year 1200, while Canterbury—one of the largest—held about 5,000 books by the year 1300. The habit of forming such collections gradually spread to private owners and to the mediaeval universities.

The number of books in monastery and cathedral libraries was increased by the efforts of the copyists: the monks in the *scriptorium*, whom the precentor drilled and kept at work, copying texts as part of their regular duties. Towards the end of the Middle Ages, in the fourteenth and fifteenth centuries, the number of books in such libraries had increased in the majority of cases from a few hundred to a few thousand. Johnson quotes from the rules of one of these libraries on the responsibilities of the librarian: 'The first duty of a librarian is to strive, in his time, as far as is possible, to increase the library committed to him'. At the time of the dissolution of the monasteries in England by Henry VIII, Johnson gives as an estimate that the eight hundred or so institutions must have contained at least 300,000 volumes. They had grown, writes John Willis Clark, 'year by year, slowly yet surely, by purchase, by gift, by bequest, by the zeal of the staff of writers'. (16)

Early college libraries were small, and they also grew very slowly. In Paris, when Robert de Sorbonne endowed a college there in 1250, he gave it his personal library; the catalogue of 1289 of the college's library listed some 1,000 titles; but a subsequent catalogue, of 1338, still lists no more than about 1,700 titles. In 1424, there were only 122 volumes in Cambridge University Library; as late as 1473, the total still had reached no more than 330 volumes. In 1375, Oriel College, Oxford, had not quite 100 volumes; in 1418, there were only 380 volumes in the library of Peterhouse College, Cambridge;

and in 1453, the library of King's College, Cambridge, was only of 174 volumes. This kind of statistical level is everywhere evident in lists of mediaeval collections of books (such as that compiled by Ernest A Savage). (17)

Also evident from such lists is the character of the collections. The preponderance of Cambridge University's collection in 1424 was theological (69), but it also included books on natural and moral philosophy (17), canon law (23), and on medicine, logic, poetry, grammar and history. In 1473, the same library contained works by Lucan, Ovid, Aristotle, Seneca, Cicero and Petrarch. At King's College, Cambridge, in 1453, the collection comprised works on philosophy, theology, medicine, astrology, mathematics, canon law, grammar, and classical and general literature including Aristotle, Plato, Cicero, Seneca, Sallust, Caesar, Ovid and Virgil.

A very basic principle of librarianship emerges clearly from any survey, no matter how cursory, of the history of the libraries of the Middle Ages. It is simply this: that libraries must grow. First of all, even the modest libraries of the Middle Ages had to achieve a certain size before they could be considered adequate by their users: the Benedictine requirement of at least one book for each of the brethren of a monastery was a declared minimum. Secondly, as with all other libraries of all other times, such libraries had to respond to and reflect the growth of learning—their religious beginnings had to be augmented by the fruits of the humanistic revival. The mediaeval universities, studying law and medicine, grammar and logic, could not be served by libraries which did not increase steadily in size and range. Library growth is too often regarded as a phenomenon of modern times, as a peculiarly contemporary problem. It is plainly nothing of the sort. The very struggles and difficulties of mediaeval libraries to grow and multiply, to keep the lamp (in Kenyon's phrase) even dimly burning in the period between the devastation of the great libraries of antiquity and the revival of learning that came with the Renaissance and the spread of printing, provide in fact a graphic illustration of the principle of growth. Library collections can never be stable or stand still.

24

3 THE AGE OF THE PRINTED BOOK

The history of libraries during the period from the end of the Middle Ages to our own times has been the age of the printed book. For five hundred years, 'printing has maintained a quasi-monopoly of the transmission or storage of infomation'. (18) Libraries have grown in size at a very great pace; since the coming of printing, they can be reckoned in thousands rather than hundreds of volumes. Before the beginning of printing an individual great work was available in maybe a hundred manuscript copies; subsequently this availability ran into hundreds of copies, then thousands, and in modern times, into millions. Edward Edwards considered that the invention of printing had the effect of 'virtually exempting books from the operation of the law which subjects all human things to decay': (19) an over-sanguine view, perhaps, in a world where the potential scale of human disaster has also escalated, but it can at least be said that the odds on a particular work surviving have certainly improved. A further point, though, is that the age of the printed book, like every other human innovation, like the clay tablets, papyrus rolls and parchment codices which preceded it, must be regarded as finite also. This present study is an historical one, rather than an essay in futurology, but even so it can be recorded that already there are a number of factual signs of a challenge to the monopoly of the printed book: audiovisual media, for example, which manage without the printed word; and the storage of data in computers. There are also signs that the economics of printing books in the traditional way are becoming increasingly problematical; and that new generations of people are becoming more and more used to absorbing information and education through media other than the printed page.

Printing as such began in Europe in the middle of the fifteenth century, when Johannes Gutenberg in Mainz, in Germany, began using movable types. By the time of the sack of Mainz in 1462, which dispersed printers and their craft all over Germany and later over Europe generally, there were already 51 printers in Germany alone. In Italy, where printing began in 1465, there were over 73 printers by the end of the century, the two most famous being Nicolas Jenson (who published more than 150 titles) and Aldo Manuzio (Aldus Manutius). In France, printing started in 1470; in Spain, 1474. In England, William Caxton, who had learned the art in Cologne and had worked in Bruges with Colard Mansion, set up his press at Westminster in 1476; and in fifteen years he produced about 100 books.

Only a few hundred copies were printed of the first *incunabula* (that is, books printed before 1500); not until the middle of the sixteenth century did the average print-run of a book go beyond 1,000 copies; and in the seventeenth and eighteenth centuries the average was between 2,000 and 3,000 copies. Even so, L Febvre and H-J Martin have estimated, (20) possibly too extravagantly, that the number of *incunabula* printed by the year 1500 was 20,000,000. And Elmer D Johnson (21) quotes an estimate that in the sixteenth century over 100,000 different books were printed in Europe, which assuming an average of 1,000 copies of each, would mean a total of 100,000,000 available during that century.

It was however in the nineteenth century that the output of printed books increased really dramatically. In the first twenty or so years of that century there was a series of inventions which revolutionised the techniques of printing, mainly to do with the mechanisation of the process—the steam press, for example. Then the era of large printings began in earnest. Robert Escarpit reminds us that when Lord Byron's *The corsair* was published in 1814, as many as 10,000 copies were sold on the day of publication; and that in the middle of the century, *Uncle Tom's cabin* sold a million and a half copies in one year.

The multiplicity of books created by the means of printing from the middle of the fifteenth century onwards had another kind of snowball effect, as Kenyon, Johnson and others have pointed out: namely, that such a diffusion of books increased literacy, promoted more widely a taste for literary culture, and opened wide the doors of learning. This in its turn led to more books being written, and so even more books being printed.

It is not difficult to appreciate the effect of such a revolution on the size of library collections, nor to understand why the birth of the printed book heralded a whole new period in their history. But it would be totally erroneous to believe that this revolution overturned or invalidated any or all of the principles of librarianship which had emerged so clearly from ancient times and from the Middle Ages. Indeed, the majority of such principles were reinforced by the revolution.

The remaining sections of this chapter examine the development in the era of the printed book of three major types of library: national libraries, public libraries, and academic libraries. Not one of these types was of course a newcomer, but all of them were able to come to a more substantial fruition and to bring into operation more fully the principles on which they had been founded. The national libraries of the modern world retrieved the baton which had been borne by the Alexandrian Library and the great library at Nineveh; the greater availability of books and the spread of literacy enabled public libraries to become truly public; and the academic libraries of the new age continued the development which had begun with the research facilities available to scholars at the Alexandrian Library, and which had re-emerged with the provision of libraries in the mediaeval colleges.

4 THE RISE OF THE NATIONAL LIBRARIES

Great national libraries are now to be found in capitals everywhere in the world: London, Paris, Vienna, Berlin, Berne, Dublin, Brussels, The Hague, Luxembourg, Florence, Athens, Madrid, Lisbon, Copenhagen, Oslo, Stockholm, Helsinki, Moscow, Leningrad, Sofia, Prague, Warsaw, Washington, Ottawa, Mexico City, Buenos Aires, Rio de Janeiro, Santiago, Lima, Cape Town, Pretoria, Jerusalem, Canberra, Tokyo.

The foundation of such libraries began in the seventeenth century (for example, the Deutsche Staatsbibliothek in Berlin, under the successive titles of Königliche Bibliothek and

Preussiche Bibliothek, dates from 1661), and continued through the eighteenth century (for example, in Florence, where the Biblioteca Magliabechiana in 1861, under the Kingdom of Italy, became the Biblioteca Nazionale) and the twentieth century (for example, Canberra and Ottawa). Some have now reached—certainly in relation to any mediaeval library, and even in relation to the Alexandrian library—a quite enormous size: the Lenin State Library in Moscow, for example, has over 22,000,000 catalogued items (including books, pamphlets and periodicals).

Elmer D Johnson has categorised these libraries as follows: 'Of all the libraries of modern Europe, the most outstanding have been the national libraries, those rapidly growing collections of "one of everything" that developed in the national capitals. Sometimes these national collections developed at the expense of other libraries, but they have generally aimed at an impossible goal of completeness, at least within the publications of their own country'. (23) A survey of their individual histories reveals many recurrent features.

The majority of national libraries are the result of the yoking together of a number of other libraries, either by gift, bequest, purchase or compulsion. The collections of Sir Hans Sloane, Sir Robert Cotton, and Edward and Robert Harley, Earls of Oxford, formed the basis of the British Museum Library. To these collections, in 1757, was added the Royal Library.

Royal libraries, indeed, figure very importantly in the history of the majority of European national libraries: in France on the outbreak of the Revolution, the Royal Library became the National; the National Library of Vienna has an intimate connection with the Imperial House of Hapsburg; and the national libraries in Stockholm and The Hague are still called 'Royal'.

Monastic libraries also found their way into the national libraries of many countries. As a result of the dispersal of books after the French Revolution, many of the contents of monastic and church libraries were received into the

28

Bibliothèque Nationale. The richest collections added to the Imperial Library at Vienna in the eighteenth century were from the Jesuits and other monasteries. The sad exception was in England, for when the monasteries were closed under Henry VIII in the sixteenth century, their libraries were destroyed or scattered, and of the 300,000 volumes which have been estimated to have been contained in the eight hundred or so monasteries, less than two per cent are known to have survived. In the words of Bishop Bale (from his preface to John Leland's *New Year's gift to King Henry VIII*), 'little respect was had to the Libraries'.

National libraries seem to have quite often benefited from revolutions. The after-effects of the French Revolution have already been mentioned: after 1789, when all religious libraries were declared national property and all the books and manuscripts therein confiscated, there followed in 1792 a general confiscation of books belonging to the nobility and other citizens who had fled France. Some 8,000,000 books were confiscated and gathered together in general book deposits in various parts of the country, and about 300,000 of the more valuable volumes ended up in the Bibliothèque Nationale. Similarly, in the period 1918 to 1923, following the Russian Revolution, a vast number of books, and indeed entire libraries, were transferred to the Lenin State Library: the most notable being the collections of the Russian Medical Society (50,000 volumes), the Moscow bookseller Chibanov (100,000 volumes), and the Counts Cheremetiev (40,000 volumes); and subsequently, on the closure of any institution, its library was transferred to the State Library, with Lenin himself taking a personal interest in the library's growth.

Also noticeable in the history of most national libraries is the contribution made by the libraries of individual great book-collectors. Mention has already been made of Sir Hans Sloane, Sir Robert Cotton, and Edward and Robert Harley, in relation to the British Museum Library. The Biblioteca Nazionale Centrale in Florence owes a massive debt to Antonio Magliabechi, the great bibliophile, who on his death in 1714 left his 30,000 volumes and 3,000 manuscripts to the people of that city. At the Library of Congress, the Librarian Ainsworth Rand Spofford filled a notable gap in that institution's collection—American history, all of Jefferson's original contributions having been lost in the ensuing fires—by purchasing the finest collection of Americana, which had been privately assembled by Peter Force.

Another recurrent theme in the growth of national libraries is the importance to each of them of the law of legal deposit. Spofford started his incumbency as Librarian of Congress in 1864 by setting out to reform the copyright law of the United States, because he 'saw the copyright collection as the base for the national library'. (24) William von Hartel, when he was appointed Director of the National Library in Vienna in 1891, sought to prevent that library from losing its place in the front rank of libraries by enforcing the law of legal deposit. At the British Museum Library in 1850, the duty of enforcing the Copyright Act was transferred from the Board of Trustees to the Keeper of Printed Books, Antonio Panizzi, giving him power of attorney; and for the next few years Panizzi's life was dominated by his determination to oblige defaulting publishers to obey the Act's provisions.

And finally, the point must be made, though it is an obvious one, that a universal characteristic of national libraries is that they are indeed nationalistic. Just as the Ptolemies made the Alexandrian Library a shrine to Hellenistic culture, and just as Ashurbanipal's library reflected the glory of his Assyrian empire, so also was the case individually with the foundation of every one of the modern national libraries. Edward Miller, for example, writes as follows on Panizzi's appointment to the British Museum Library: 'The new Keeper's thoughts were mainly engaged . . . on how to make his library supreme, not only in Great Britain, but throughout the world. "This emphatically *British* library", he wrote, "ought to be directed most particularly to British works and to works relating to the British Empire, its religious, political and literary as well as scientific history, its laws, its institutions, commerce, arts, etc. The rarer and more expensive a work of this description is the more . . . efforts ought to be made to secure it for the Library". Panizzi speaks with the very voice of High Victorian patriotism.' (25)

Among the modern national libraries, the British Museum Library and the Library of Congress are certainly regarded as two of the most outstanding, and in connection with them it will be instructive to follow the precept of Edward Edwards referred to in the first chapter of this book: namely, to examine the 'biography' of each, though necessarily very briefly.

The British Museum Library was not officially founded until 1753, but there had been earlier abortive proposals for a national library. The first proposal on record was made in 1556 by John Dee, a scientist, astrologer and book-collector, who presented to Queen Mary a 'supplication' for a 'Library Royal'. (26) In the following reign a petition was drafted by Robert Cotton, John Doddridge and James Lee, for a 'Library of Queen Elizabeth', but this petition appears never to have been presented. Dr Richard Bently, Royal Librarian under William III, Anne, George I and George II, also devised (in 1697) a proposal for building a Royal Library and establishing it by Act of Parliament.

In the end, though, it was the bequest of Sir Hans Sloane (1660-1753), physician to George II and president of the Royal Society, which brought about the foundation in England of a national library. Sloane's will directed his trustees to offer his collections—which included, as well as specimens in the fields of botany, zoology, and mineralogy, some 40,000 printed books and 3,500 manuscripts—to the Crown or to Parliament for £20,000, a sum much less than their true value. After much hesitation, an Act of Parliament was passed in 1753 to purchase Sloane's collections, and along with them, the manuscript collection of Robert and Edward Harley, Earls of Oxford; and for these two collections, and for Sir Robert Cotton's collection of historical manuscripts (which had already been transferred to the Crown in 1700), to provide a repository.

The first such repository was found in 1755, at Montague House, Bloomsbury, the home of the second Duke of Montague, who died in 1749. In 1757, George II presented the Royal Library of the kings of England (from Edward IV to George II), and this brought with it the right of a free copy of all books entered at Stationer's Hall. The 'British Museum' was first opened to the public on January 15 1759.

In the 1820s, according to Edward Edwards, (27) the Library possessed about 115,000 volumes. When Antonio Panizzi became Keeper of Printed Books in 1837, he found that this number has been virtually doubled, mainly by the purchase in 1823 from George IV of the royal library of George III. Under Panizzi's care, by 1856, the number of printed books had reached 560,000.

The first wing of a new building for the Library was completed in 1828, designed by Sir Robert Smirke in the Greek style. Later, in 1852, on the basis of rough sketches by Panizzi, the celebrated round Reading Room was designed by Sir Robert's brother, Sydney Smirke. The Reading Room—a circular reading area surrounded by books in iron stacks—was begun in 1854 and opened in 1857.

Much more significant though, was the librarianship of Antonio Panizzi. 'The British Museum Library as most of us have known it', wrote Sir Frank Francis, 'is Panizzi's creation'. (28)

Panizzi was appointed Assistant Librarian at the British Museum in 1831, and his first duties were in the field of cataloguing. In 1837, he was appointed Keeper of Printed Books, and he set out, as recorded earlier in this section on national libraries, to make the Library supreme not only in Great Britain but throughout the world. He secured from the Treasury a book grant of £10,000 per annum, which was a remarkable achievement. He greatly improved and increased the Library's holdings of foreign books by employing active and zealous agents throughout Europe and in the United States. And, as noted earlier, he enforced the law of legal deposit: prior to his time, only two-fifths of the books to which the Museum was entitled were being received, since publishers were up to every trick and device to evade the provisions of the Act. Panizzi actually went so far as to prosecute defaulters, despite storms of abuse and indignation, and pursued publishers in Wales, Scotland and Ireland as well as in England. It was hard, wounding work, but he was successful. In May 1857, when the new Reading Room was formally opened, it was truly—in Edward Miller's words (29)—'Panizzi's hour': in that year, Panizzi was no longer merely the Keeper of Printed Books, but Principal Librarian.

Panizzi laid the foundations for a century of solid growth, so that now, in the 1970s, the stock of the Library for which he was responsible at such a key period, stands at over 8,000,000 printed books and 130,000 manuscripts.

In 1972, the British Library Act was passed, whereby from April 1 1973, following the recommendations of the 1969 report of the National Libraries Committee (under the chairmanship of Sir Frederick Dainton), the various national library institutions in England were brought together to form the British Library: the British Museum Library becoming the Reference Division, the National Central Library and the National Lending Library for Science and Technology becoming the Lending Division, and the British National Bibliography becoming the Bibliographic Services Division.

The First Annual Report of the British Library, 1973-74, (30) states the first purpose of the newly-christened Reference Division to be: 'to collect, by purchase, gift and exchange, not only all British books and such British manuscripts and papers as are appropriate, but as much as possible of the world's important printed material in all subject fields, and manuscripts of foreign origin in certain specialist fields'. At the risk of labouring the point, it must be remarked again, that the pedigree of such a statement is a very long one, and the basic principle of librarianship that informs it is getting on for three thousand years' old.

The Library of Congress provides even more striking statistics of growth.

Despite a modest and rather chequered beginning, it now contains 16,000,000 books and 30,000,000 manuscripts. It also has 250,000 gramophone records, 100,000 reels of film, and in the words of its most recent historian, Charles A Goodrum, (31) 'endless cases of maps, photographs, volumes in Braille, rolls of microfilm, papyri, magnetic tape, and every other form of preserved thought'. All told it contains more than 64,000,000 items; it has, again in Goodrum's words, 'almost by accident, managed to accumulate almost all of man's recorded knowledge in one place'.

The Library of Congress was formally founded in 1800. By 1807, its total collection was approaching 3,000 volumes. In 1814, however, British soldiers marched into Washington and set fire to the Capitol, destroying the Library. The following summer, the Library was re-started by the purchase of the library of ex-President Thomas Jefferson, a collection of 6,487 volumes. By 1836, the Library had grown to 24,000 volumes.

A further set-back occurred in 1851, when a fire destroyed 35,000 of the Library's volumes and almost all of its map collection. There had been an earlier fire, in 1825, but that had been extinguished before any substantial loss. By 1863, the Library held 79,214 volumes.

In 1864, President Lincoln appointed Ainsworth Rand Spofford as sixth Librarian of Congress. Goodrum describes Spofford as 'the Cecil Rhodes of the institution, an empire builder in the finest Victorian tradition'. Spofford dedicated his thirty-three years as Librarian to making the Library of Congress the national library.

As noted earlier in this section, Spofford set out to reform the copyright law of the United States. A previous act, that of 1846, had required the deposit of three copies of every work: one to the State Department, one to the Smithsonian Institution, and one to the Library of Congress. The copyright law of 1870, however, required that two copies of every publication be sent to the Librarian of Congress within ten days of its publication, with penalties for failing to comply. In the subsequent twenty-five years, the Library received

371,636 books, 257,153 magazines, 289,617 pieces of music, 73,817 photographs, 95,249 prints, and 48,048 maps. Spofford also recovered precious deposits to the Departments of State and Interior; and in addition, arranged to be the recipient of exchange material generated by the publications of the Smithsonian—an arrangement which has since brought to the Library of Congress over 2,000,000 items in the Smithsonian Deposit. At the same time as all of this, Spofford pursued specific collections, such as the Peter Force collection of Americana mentioned earlier.

By the 1870s Spofford had acute space problems, and so began his long struggle to obtain a building capable of housing his vast accumulation. It took him fifteen years to get a law passed and an appropriation for its construction, and eleven years more to build it. 'Spofford's library', writes Goodrum, 'clearly became a personal monument to his singleness of purpose'. The building, built for Spofford by General Thomas Casey, Chief of the Army Corps of Engineers, was immense for its day. It was opened in 1897, just after Spofford had been replaced as Librarian of Congress by John Russell Young (appointed by President William McKinley, inaugurated 1897). Goodrum remarks that of the librarian's three duties—'acquisition, cataloguing, and reference'—Spofford had an 'overpreoccupation' with the first, to the neglect of the two others. Even on the basis of the brief history of national libraries which has been offered here, it would however seem that Spofford knew best: by so massively founding the collections of the Library of Congress between 1864 and 1897, he made that Library what it is today. It was left to his successors—Herbert Putnam (Librarian for forty years) and Archibald MacLeish (Librarian 1939-1944), in particular—to worry about cataloguing, organisation, and service; but with such a foundation, the Library was bound to grow to its present eminence.

5. THE PROVISION OF PUBLIC LIBRARIES
The history of public libraries, in relation to the history of the principles of librarianship, has more to do with the

principles of access than with those principles which govern the size and content of collections. Even so, the history of the provision of public library collections cannot be passed over in this chapter completely.

As will be seen in a subsequent chapter, the history of public access to libraries is a long one, but public libraries in the fullest sense are a development of the nineteenth and twentieth centuries, and belong essentially to the age of the printed book, the rise of democracy, and the spread of popular education. As Sir Frederic Kenyon remarked, (32) since the early nineteenth century 'private libraries have been increasingly over-shadowed by the public ones, which absorb continually and never disgorge'. He describes the nineteenth century as the period of 'the growth of a new type of library, the public library supported out of public funds', and of course, the period also of the growth of the great national collections.

The development of the public library illustrates very clearly a particular principle of librarianship: namely, that libraries are created by society. The task of promoting libraries might fall on the shoulders of a few enlightened and inspired individuals, but the seeds such individuals scatter have to fall on receptive ground if they are to come to fruition. The rise of democracy meant that libraries could no longer be reserved for an elite, and the spread of education required the intellectual sustenance that libraries provide. The provision of public libraries was inevitable.

Even so, in England it was not until 1850 that, as a result of the joint exertions of William Ewart and Edward Edwards, an Act was passed for (in Edwards's own words) the 'founding, maintaining, and administering FREE LIBRARIES for the British people, by a permanent rate, equably levied and responsibly expended'. (33) The 1850 Public Libraries Act empowered Town Councils of towns with a population of 10,000 to provide libraries to which the public should be admitted without charge, and to levy a half-penny rate for the purpose. In 1855, the population limit was lowered to 5,000;

authority was given to purchase books instead of relying upon gifts; and the maximum rate was raised to one penny. Not until 1919 was the penny rate restriction removed.

The first public library in London, apart from the Guild-hall, was Westminster, founded in 1857. The big impetus in Britain came after 1890, when Andrew Carnegie, between 1897 and 1913, made gifts amounting to one and three-quarter million pounds for the building and equipment of public libraries. Such libraries were confined to the urban areas until the first world war, but in 1915, following the report to the Carnegie Trustees prepared by Professor W G S Adams, the system was extended to the rural areas. Stafford-shire was the first authority to establish a County Library, in 1916. Eventually the whole population of Great Britain was included within the area of some library authority whose duty was to supply it with books.

Edwards records that within ten or eleven years of the operation of the 1850 Act, some 260,000 volumes were secured for public use and made thoroughly accessible, each volume on average being used ten times each year, and renewed when worn out. Thomas Kelly tells us, (34) though, that in 1886, only four public libraries—Manchester, Birmingham, Leeds and Liverpool—had a bookstock of more than 100,000 volumes. Because of the limitation of the penny rate, growth was slow, but by 1913-14, Manchester and Birmingham both exceeded 400,000 volumes, and Leeds and Liverpool 300,000 volumes. Often there was the problem of 'overbuilding'—that is, the upkeep of a large building (perhaps provided by a Carnegie grant) absorbed most of the proceeds from the penny rate, leaving little for book purchase. Nevertheless, by 1923-24, Manchester had 570,000 books, Birmingham 550,000, Leeds 359,000, and Liverpool 411,000. By 1935, Manchester had 735,000 volumes, Birmingham 925,000, Leeds 373,000, and Liverpool 589,000. In the later 1960s, according to Elmer D Johnson, (35) the public libraries of Britain as a whole contained over 80,000,000 volumes. By the early 1970s, the stocks of the four large public libraries whose individual growth has been traced so far, were as follows: (36) Manchester—in the adult lending collections 904,863 volumes; in the reference collections, 694,542 volumes; and in the junior library collections, 110,724 volumes. The corresponding figures in the early 1970s were, for Birmingham, 1,003,546, 863,045, and 270,909; for Leeds, 479,616, 416,457, and 75,724; and for Liverpool, 834,972, 1,148,443, and 261,606.

The development of public libraries in the rest of Europe, except for the Scandinavian countries, has been altogether slower. In the United States, however, and in Canada also, they have flourished. In terms of chronology, the founding of American public libraries and British public libraries were coeval. Indeed it is Boston Public Library, founded in 1852, which can claim to be the oldest free municipal library supported by taxation in any city in the world.

The need of American society for libraries (which will be explored in more detail in chapter four) showed itself early, but it was in the period between 1820 and 1850 that the greatest efforts were made to achieve a 'more abundant provision of libraries'. (37) In that period there were developed libraries for apprentices and mechanics; libraries for young men pursuing a mercantile or commercial career; and 'young men's associations' which provided libraries for their members. Then came the idea of a system of small libraries attached to the common schools.

It was in 1848 that the city of Boston was empowered by law to establish and maintain a public library. However, though by 1876 (when the American Library Association was formed) no less than sixteen states had passed legislation authorising the maintenance of libraries by cities and towns, among cities of more than 100,000 inhabitants a free public circulating library had been established in only six—Boston in 1852, Detroit in 1865, Cincinnati in 1867, Cleveland in 1868, Louisville in 1871, and Chicago in 1872.

In terms of growth, it is worth looking at the stock figures on these six libraries just over a hundred years later. By

1974, (38) Boston had 3,092,424 volumes; Detroit 2,185,757 volumes; Cincinnati, 2,917,547 volumes; Cleveland, over 3,000,000 volumes; Louisville, 946,000 volumes; and Chicago, 5,193,616 volumes. And by the same year, the New York Public Library, though not founded until 1895, contained 8,426,684 volumes: truly the coming of age of the printed book.

6 THE GROWTH OF UNIVERSITY LIBRARIES
The growth of university libraries, in the age of the printed book, has followed much the same path as that of national libraries and public libraries: modest beginnings progressing to a kind of gigantism, with the more extreme version of the development taking place in the United States. The major academic libraries—Harvard, the Bodleian, and the Library of the USSR Academy of Sciences in Leningrad, for example—now rival the great national libraries in the range and quality of their collections. Harvard has as many books as the British Library Reference Division (formerly the British Museum Library). The Bodleian, like the British Library, enjoys the considerable privilege of being a legal deposit library. The Library of the USSR Academy of Sciences in Leningrad is, with its collection of 13,800,000 volumes, not shamed even by a comparison with the Library of Congress.

The beginnings were indeed modest. In Europe, before 1500, there were some seventy-five universities. Johnson has explained (39) that, unlike the monastery libraries, where acquisitions were gained by copying, early college libraries grew largely through donations: 'Endowed funds were also given to universities for the purchase of books or the upkeep of libraries, and there is also evidence that library fees were collected from students in some cases'.

The Bodleian, founded at Oxford in 1602 by Sir Thomas Bodley, is one of England's oldest and most important libraries. Bodley, recounts E A Savage, (40) 'employed John Bill, the bookseller, to visit regularly the book mart at Frankfurt, and to travel in the Low Countries, France, Germany,

Italy, and Spain to collect books. From the start Bodley's contained books, not only in the classical, Hebrew, and European languages, but in Ethiopic, Arabic, Brazilian, Chinese, Mexican and Peruvian; and Bodley was even anxious to have an agent in the Near East. And when, in the study of library history, you come across such a passage as the following by Bodley, in which he dreams of the library to be, are we not encouraged and sustained? The new library, he writes, "may perhaps in tyme to come, proue a notable treasure for the multitude of volumes; an excellent benefit for the vse and ease of students: and a singuler ornament to the Vniuersity" '. By 1620, the Bodleian possessed 16,000 volumes; by 1700, nearly 30,000 volumes. Now, in the mid-1970s, it has about 3,500,000 printed books, and 50,000 manuscripts.

Cambridge University Library had only 300 printed books and 150 manuscripts in 1582. By 1650, it contained some 1,000 books and 400 manuscripts. Two and a half centuries later, in 1900, its collections were close to 1,000,000 volumes. Now, in the mid-1970s, it too has about 3,000,000 volumes.

Oxford and Cambridge dominate in size the British university library scene. After their 3,000,000 volume level, the next group—Glasgow, Edinburgh, Leeds, Birmingham, London —each contain approximately 1,000,000 volumes. The exception is Manchester University Library, which following its merger with the John Rylands Library, now can claim a bookstock of some 2,000,000 volumes. The remaining univeristy libraries in Britain are below the 1,000,000-volume mark, and indeed for most, the 500,000-volume level is still a significant one.

The real giants, as may be expected, are to be found in the United States. The oldest university library, Harvard, founded in 1638, had 12,000 volumes by the 1780s. In 1831, the figure was 39,605 volumes; in 1849, 96,200 volumes; in 1876, 227,650 volumes; in 1900, 560,000 volumes; in 1925, 2,416,500 volumes; and in 1938, 3,941,359. The significance of these figures, as Fremont Rider explains, (41) is that they show that in common with other vigorously-growing American university libraries, Harvard is doubling in size every sixteen years or so. It was this statistical fact which had most to do with the preoccupation of librarians, over the past few decades, with the problems of size: a topic which will be treated in the next, and final, section of the present chapter.

Harvard, by the mid 1970s, was well on the way to 9,000,000 volumes. Yale, founded in 1701, had 114,200 volumes in 1876; these one hundred years later, its collections amount approximately to 6,000,000 volumes. Princeton, founded in 1746, had 41,500 volumes in 1876; now that library has some 3,000,000 volumes. Berkeley, though not founded until 1868, already has a total of 13,500,000 volumes. Stanford, founded in 1885, has 3,850,000 volumes. Chicago, founded in 1892, is approaching 3,500,000 volumes. Robert B Downs (42) summed up this remarkable state of growth by pointing out that the number of volumes in the research libraries of the United States went from 138,228,000 volumes in 1935, to 280,860,000 volumes in 1955, and then to 791,696,000 volumes in 1973—that is, nearly tripling in the past two decades.

7 THE PROBLEMS OF SIZE

On the basis of the foregoing evidence there is plainly no denying the principle that libraries must grow. What the world of librarianship now seems to be awaiting is the emergence of some corollary principle or principles which meet the problems of seemingly infinite and massive growth in every type of major library. However, incredible though it may appear, library history seems to indicate that such an expectation may be premature. Libraries do not survive forever: the Alexandrian Library, after all, disappeared; and just about all the books in the eight hundred or so mediaeval religious libraries in Britain were destroyed. Also, the clay tablet, the papyrus roll, and the parchment codex were all, in turn and in time, overtaken: there is no logical reason why the printed book should not likewise be superseded. The other assumption is that our present social, political and economic order which permits and promotes the growth of libraries, will continue securely for ever more: this patently can only be an assumption.

But, nevertheless, the problems of size are with us. In the article on library architecture in the current edition of the *Encyclopaedia Britannica* (43) there is the comment: 'It is commonly held that, on present showing, research library collections are doubling in size every 16 to 20 years—even the largest national libraries are increasing at this rate. Such an increase can hardly be supported indefinitely . . . ' Statistics of growth, almost guaranteed to alarm, are presented on every side: Robert B Downs, for example, who provided the figures on the growth of research libraries quoted at the end of the previous section of this chapter, also recorded (44) that the libraries in the New York City area held 12,910,623 volumes in 1935; that by 1955, this figure had grown to 24,688,777 volumes; and that in 1973, it stood at 47,305,190 volumes.

Edward Edwards (45) confronted this problem more than a hundred years ago, but was not dismayed by it. He had observed that when the new buildings of the British Museum were first planned (1822-23), the actual number of volumes in the Library (both of manuscript and printed books together) was under 200,000, but that at the time of his writing *Memoirs of libraries* (1859), the collections exceeded 600,000 volumes, and the average annual intake was approaching 20,000 volumes. He commented: 'That a National Library should treble its contents within less than a third of a century —unassisted by any of those extraordinary opportunities which have elsewhere been afforded by revolutions or conquests—was wholly without precedent'. He considered, though, that national libraries should indeed be storehouses, 'encyclopaedical', containing not only the monuments of literature, but ephemera also: 'To a great National Library, indeed, all kinds and varieties of books are welcome, and may wisely be sought for. But a Library of this class is rather a growth than a formation.'

42

Edwards was not unaware of the problems such a policy might create. 'It may, doubtless, be somewhat startling,' he wrote, 'to contemplate the kind of receptacles which will by and bye be required for this comprehensive storing up of both the literature, and the historic raw-material, as well of the present as of past ages.' But he remained convinced that, 'For the useful and honourable craft of "book-makers", we must continue to have vast miscellaneous store-houses, and the more extensive these are, the larger will be the proportion borne by the mere books of reference to the aggregate numbers, and the larger also will be the proportion of the "trash" . . . '

However, the 'great repositories' aside, Edwards was not advocating wide-ranging and limitless growth for all types of library. His belief was that there is also a need for libraries 'of narrower aims and more specific character', and he pointed out that professional libraries in fields such as law and medicine are the easiest of these to form. More difficult, he thought, were Provincial and Town Libraries, which while having 'a distinctly popular and educational character', yet aimed to meet the requirements and 'subserve the users' of all classes of the population. He states that those who set out to form a Library for the Public should have clear ideas of 'the aims with which it is established', of the studies which it is 'more especially intended to facilitate', and of 'the probable requirements' of the majority of the people who will use it. He was aware that the precise formulation and interpretation of such a policy would not be easy, and he made an attempt to indicate certain areas of collection—specifically, and first: all possible material on the locality of the library, covering all aspects and including works printed locally; then, particular concentration on some special subjects, the choice of which would depend on 'the preferences of the promoters of the Library', the character and extent of neighbouring libraries, the amount of funds available for purchases, and many other factors; but in any event, there ought to be at least 'some one important subject' chosen, upon which the Library should have 'a systematic *Collection*', rather than 'a mere chance aggregation'.

At no point is Edwards talking of any limitation of size. His concern is with the relevance of library collections, not their scale. He plainly accepts the principle that libraries must grow; and equally plainly, he subscribes to the 'Great Wen' principle of national libraries: namely, that every national publication should find its way into the national library, even if it will be consulted only infrequently ('the larger will be the proportion borne by the mere books of reference'), and even if it be considered of dubious value ('trash'). The essence of his comment on 'mere books of reference' was taken up a century later by Fremont Rider, as will be discussed shortly. His point about the proportion of 'trash' was answered two centuries before him, by Gabriel Naudé, who in his *Avis pour dresser une bibliothèque* (1627), wrote: 'There is nothing which renders a Library more recommendable, than when every man finds in it that which he is in search of, and could nowhere else encounter; this being a perfect Maxime, that there is no Book whatsoever, be it never so bad or decried, but may in time be sought by some person or other'. (46) Naudé's view of 'trash' was also supported independently in the twentieth century by Henry Evelyn Bliss, when he wrote: 'Our book-stacks are crowded with dead books and those soon to die. Our catalogues are encumbered with their cards in complicated arrangements. In a few decades much of this material will be in decay; much of it will be useless. Yet most of it should be stored somewhere. Some of it may be precious some day. Some of it, never precious, will have occasional readers.' (47) A contrary view, however, was expressed by Raymond Irwin, (48) also in the twentieth century: Irwin was worried by the amount of 'chaff', as opposed to 'grain', in our national libraries as a result of legal deposit. He talks of 'a vast and rapidly growing accumulation of chaff which is cherished with all the devotion due to works of merit', and observes that the 'good sense of this policy is perhaps questionable, and a bolder solution of the problem might be recommended'. But then he goes on to suggest, rather conjecturally, that what has come down to us through the ages, 'through the storms of more than two millenniums', has been the result of a 'guiding hand'. He does not specify what kind of guiding hand he means, but the inference must be that he is referring to a divine one. In brief, as far as 'chaff' (or 'trash') is concerned, Irwin wants to leave 'the winnowing to Time'.

Now it may seem to offer a contradiction to Edwards's modest statements of policy regarding the collections of a Town Library, that, as was noted in an earlier section of this chapter, the New York Public Library by 1974 contained 8,426,684 volumes. But New York is a cosmopolitan city of more than 8,000,000 people, with a vast range of commercial, technical, educational, social, recreational and artistic interests; and Edwards's recommendation that a Library for the Public should meet the requirements and subserve the uses of all classes of the population could surely be considered to require at least one book per head.

Another voice continuing, despite the greatly-increased size of present library collections, to support the principle that libraries must nevertheless still grow, was that of Ernest A Savage, who wrote: (49) 'The oldest libraries are the best if they have been added to continuously from their foundation to the present day'. Savage's emphasis on continuity was a valid one, along with its corollary that libraries should be as much concerned with the needs of future generations as with contemporary needs. Contemporary strains on resources ought not necessarily to be allowed to pre-empt the future. As Savage also commented: 'But I doubt whether we have yet learned how broadly based many of the old libraries were; how eager their founders or librarians were to get books of all kinds, even those for which they could see no immediate use'.

Curiously, in our own time, it was a defender of the growth of libraries who collected some of the statistics which caused the general alarm about the size of contemporary collections. In his book *The scholar and the future of the research library*

(1944), Fremont Rider examined the problems posed by 'the astonishing growth of our great research libraries.' It was he who noted that American research libraries, over the three centuries since they began, have been doubling in size every sixteen years, and that obviously therefore there 'is going to come a time when some sort of an *impasse* begins to impend very rapidly indeed'.

As one illustration of his thesis, Rider looks at the growth of the library collections of Yale University. In the early part of the eighteenth century, Yale had about 1,000 volumes. Doubling in size as it did approximately every sixteen years, it had accumulated 2,748,000 volumes by 1938. Calculating its future growth on the same statistical basis, Yale will have some 200,000,000 volumes by the year 2040, occupying over 6,000 miles of shelving.

Rider's reaction to these his own calculations is no different from his predecessors at the Alexandrian Library, nor in the monastic libraries: he believes that libraries must nevertheless be allowed to grow. His main argument is that there has always existed a direct statistical correlation 'between the educational effectiveness of a college and the growth of its library': thus, if you want to have a strong college, you must have a library which doubles in size every sixteen years. Only if an educational institution is stagnant will this growth not take place.

He concedes that a slackening of this rate of growth is 're-motely possible', but not in the forseeable future. Here the reader of the present work might consider the relevant comments in the earlier general section on the age of the printed book: the end of the cheap book now appears to be in sight, for example; publishing output may possibly be reduced for economic reasons; and library funds may not grow so fast because of world-wide economic recessions. The economic future of libraries is admittedly only conjectural: the libraries on which Rider bases his statistical preductions have, after all, successfully weathered three centuries of economic cycles. But there are also, as was pointed out earlier, other major

46

factors which could come into play: political and social ones (and here library history can provide examples of extreme disaster), and technological changes (which could conceivably supersede the printed book).

Rider is at pains to make clear that his main thesis relates not to public libraries, nor to college libraries, but to 'research libraries', 'the store-up knowledge of the race', 'the building blocks of civilization'. He does not consider that 'everything needs to be preserved everywhere'. He categorises research materials as 'not read'—but merely referred to or consulted; and as being 'comparatively little used'—since researchers are 'always working on intellectual frontiers'. He also notes that research materials are used only by 'those who have gained a certain level of intellectual competency': that is, scholars, and what is more, only those scholars in a particular speciality.

In sum, Rider identifies the characteristics of research library materials as being first, that the use made of them is relatively short; second, that they are used relatively infrequently; and third, that there is relatively high specialisation in their use. As a consequence, such materials require a quite different approach in cataloguing, binding and housing. It is on the basis of this diagnosis that Rider considers the problems arising from the growth of the great research collections.

He tackles first the idea of keeping down the size of libraries by 'weeding'. He points out, to start with, that it is impossible to deny research materials to any teaching institution: you cannot have just a 'teaching' collection, otherwise the teachers will grow stale. Then he examines the notion of a 'revolving collection'—the 'Fixed-number-of-volumes' theory: but is quick to observe that the rock on which this always founders is 'continuations'—that is, continuing sets of periodicals, government documents, transactions of societies, and so on. According to his argument, you cannot throw away the earlier volumes of the Early English Text Society just to keep the size of a library constant.

A further argument advanced by Rider against the 'fixed-number-of-volumes' theory is that colleges and institutions of learning tend themselves to grow, and therefore their libraries must grow in keeping with them. Human knowledge also grows all the time. This growth cannot be met by a library borrowing from other libraries, since borrowing rather than owning is not always an economical policy. He also notes that a 'selective research library' is a contradiction in terms. Rider comments on another aspect of the idea of keeping down a library's size by 'weeding': namely, that with any such policy there is 'conjoined the assumption' that there will exist other libraries which will still hold all the materials—which will, in Rider's phrase, 'hold the research bag'. And he calculates that the number of such 'top libraries' which would have to be available in the United States alone would not be small.

He then discusses the idea of a major research library providing itself with a 'storage warehouse', into which it could 'weed' an increasing proportion of its bookstock. Rider observes that in his opinion all such an arrangement points to is inefficient library design in the first place. It fixes the size of the library building, but not the size of the library. Eventually, under such an arrangement, the so-called 'warehouse' will become the library; and the library itself will become an architectural monument, or (in a university), an undergraduate library. He categorises all such ventures into savings on storage costs as 'transfers, or avoidances, or postponements, of cost' rather than real attempts to face the problem.

Rider also deals with inter-library cooperation as a possible solution to the problems of library growth. He starts with 'union catalogue cooperation': the resources of a number of research libraries being recorded in one overall catalogue. But he points out that only the 'self-denial' aspect of such a scheme can have any effect on growth: that is, a library does not buy a particular book because the union catalogue reveals that there is a copy elsewhere. He then goes on to consider 'division-of-fields cooperation': the elimination of unnecessary duplicative growth between the research libraries of any given area by means of an agreed-to division, amongst themselves, of specific subject fields of acquisitions. In those subject fields which a library selects as its own, the library is usually asked to agree to acquire everything. Rider observes that there are very real difficulties of division and allocation, but that a more profound problem is that any thorough-going division of fields cannot remain just a library matter: it has serious implications for the college. Eventually, and logically, one would not have college and university libraries based on local curricular requirements, but college curricula (and faculty and student bodies) based on local library holdings.

Rider also mentions the device of regional amalgamations of libraries, especially regional storage warehouses. Of the latter he does say that for the libraries co-operating 'it postpones materially the impact of cumulative growth, for it eliminates all duplicative waste among themselves'; but again, he notes, it raises the problem that for some readers it is actually moving their 'library' further away from them. The other fact is that 'the benefits of cooperation cannot be secured without the sacrifice of a certain amount of local autonomy'.

Rider concludes that all attempts to meet the problem of library growth by inter-library cooperation have one common denominator: 'they propose to solve it, in one way or another, by taking the scholar's books away from him'. In 'weeding-out' this is blatant and permanent; in 'storage warehousing', it is taking them only a short distance away; in 'dividing-up-fields', the materials are being taken a long way away, and 'for keeps'.

He stresses the scholar's need for 'book immediateness', since research use tends to be casual, short, and often unanticipated. But to do that forever, he says, books must be cheap, cataloguing must be cheap, binding must be cheap, and book storage must be cheap. In his particular opinion therefore, it is a four-part problem; and what is needed for its solution is a breakthrough in technique.

The subtitle of Rider's book is 'a problem and its solution'. His diagnosis of the problem is sound, and his support for the principle that libraries must grow is born out by twenty-five centuries of library history. But his solution has not yet found favour on the scale he suggested. In brief, Rider proposed ingeniously that microcards, combining the catalogue card entry for a book with, on the reverse of that card, the book in microform, should constitute the future contents of the great research libraries. His choice of technological means may not have been exactly right, but his contribution to the debate on the problems of size was a very positive and valuable one.

References

1 JOSEPHUS: *Jewish antiquities*, Book XII, trans by R Marcus (Loeb), 1943.

2 PARSONS, E A: *The Alexandrian Library*, 1952.

3 FRASER, P M: *Ptolemaic Alexandria*, vol 1, 1972.

4 FRASER, P M: *op cit*, 3.

5 FRASER, P M: *op cit*, 3.

6 EDWARDS, E: *Libraries and founders of libraries*, 1865.

7 JOHNSON, E D: *History of libraries in the Western world* 2nd ed, 1970.

8 EDWARDS, E: *op cit*, 6.

9 BLADES, W: *The enemies of books*, 1902.

10 PARSONS, E A: *op cit*, 2.

11 FRASER, P M: *op cit*, 3.

12 JOHNSON, E D: *op cit*, 7.

13 JOHNSON, E D: *op cit*, 7.

14 KENYON, Sir F: *Libraries and museums*, 1930.

15 NORRIS, D M: *A history of cataloguing*, 1939.

16 CLARK, J W: *The care of books*, 1901.

17 SAVAGE, E A: *Old English libraries*, 1911.

18 LECHÈNE, R: article on printing in *Encyclopaedia Britannica*, 15th ed, 1974.

19 EDWARDS, E: *op cit*, 6.

20 Quoted in ESCARPIT, R: *The book revolution*, 1966.

21 JOHNSON, E D: *op cit*, 7.

22 ESCARPIT, R: *op cit*, 20.

23 JOHNSON, E D: *op cit*, 7.

24 GOODRUM, C A: *The Library of Congress*, 1974.

25 MILLER, E: *Prince of librarians*, 1967.

26 Quoted in RAWLINGS, G B: *The British Museum Library*, 1916.

27 EDWARDS, E: *op cit*, 6.

28 Introduction to MILLER, E: *op cit*, 25.

29 MILLER, E: *op cit*, 25.

30 BRITISH LIBRARY: *First annual report, 1973-74*.

31 GOODRUM, C A: *op cit*, 24.

32 KENYON, *Sir* F: *op cit*, 14.

33 EDWARDS, E: *op cit*, 6.

34 KELLY, T: *A history of public libraries in Great Britain*, 1973.

35 JOHNSON, E D: *op cit*, 7.

36 *The libraries, museums and art galleries year book*, 1971.

37 THOMPSON, C S: *Evolution of the American public library*, 1952.

38 *The world of learning, 1974-75*, vol 2, 1974.

39 JOHNSON, E D: *op cit*, 7.

40 Introduction to THORNTON, J L: *The chronology of librarianship*, 1941.

41 RIDER, F: *The scholar and the future of the research library*, 1944.

42 DOWNS, R B: *Library resources in the United States College and research libraries*, March 1974.

43 *Encyclopaedia Britannica*, 15th ed, 1974.

44 DOWNS, R B: *op cit*, 42.

45 EDWARDS, E: *Memoirs of libraries*, 1859.

46 Quoted in IRWIN, R: *The origins of the English library*, 1958.

47 BLISS, H E: *The organization of knowledge in libraries and the subject-approach to books*, 2nd ed, 1939.

48 IRWIN, R: *The heritage of the English library*, 1964.

49 SAVAGE, E A: *op cit*, 40.

CHAPTER THREE

The responsibility for conservation

1 THE CURATORIAL FUNCTION

The curatorial function of librarians—the responsibility to look after the materials in their care—has been acknowledged and accepted from the earliest days of libraries. Indeed, the librarian-dragon jealously guarding his (or her) precious book-hoard is a familiar caricature, and it reflects an attitude which was well expressed by William Blades: 'Looked at rightly, the possession of any old book is a sacred trust, which a conscientious owner or guardian would as soon think of ignoring as a parent would of neglecting his child. An old book, whatever its subject or internal merits, is truly a portion of the national history; we may imitate it and print it in fac-simile, but we can never exactly reproduce it; and as an historical document it should be carefully preserved.' (1)

Conservation of a very positive kind was practised in both Ashurbanipal's library at Nineveh and in the Alexandrian Library. The scribes at Nineveh 'were kept busily employed . . . in inscribing new editions of older works'. (2) It was the custom in the clay tablet libraries of Babylonia and Assyria, according to James Westfall Thompson, (3) 'to have fresh copies made, from time to time, from the originals, which might have become defaced by usage, or their edges worn or nicked'. In the Alexandrian Library similarly, literature was saved and preserved. Raymond Irwin states (4) that papyrus was very perishable and that the conservation of texts was only achieved by 'constant reproduction'.

In the monastic libraries of the Middle Ages, as was noted in the previous chapter, the brethren in the *scriptoria* were likewise engaged. In addition, extreme care was exercised in the handling of the precious codices. John Willis Clarke (5) tells us that the very mode of holding a manuscript was prescribed by general custom, and he quotes in illustration an Order of the General Benedictine Chapter: 'When the religious are engaged in reading in cloister or in church, they shall if possible hold the books in their left hands, wrapped in the sleeve of their tunics, and resting on their knees; their right hands shall be uncovered with which to hold and turn the leaves of the aforesaid books'. He also relates that in the religious house at Monte Cassino, the possession of handkerchiefs (normally regarded as effeminate) was excused on the ground that they would be useful for wrapping round the manuscripts which the brethren handled. And he translates a relevant note from a fourteenth century manuscript in the same library: 'Whoever pursues his studies in this book, should be careful to handle the leaves gently and delicately, so as to avoid tearing them by reason of their thinness; and let him imitate the example of Jesus Christ who, when he had quietly opened the book of Isaiah and read therein attentively, rolled it up with reverence, and gave it again to the minister'.

Early librarians, like their successors, were of course very concerned by negligence and theft. Clark recounts that when in 1475 Sixtus IV appointed Bartolommeo Platina as Librarian of the Vatican Library, it was evident that that Library had suffered considerably from the negligence of those in whose charge it had formerly been; many volumes were missing and those remaining were in a poor condition. Platina engaged a binder and set him to work repairing and making good, while Sixtus IV issued a Bull of exceptional severity which, after declaring that 'certain ecclesiastical and secular persons, having no fear of God before their eyes, had taken sundry volumes in theology and other faculties from the library, which volumes they still presume rashly and maliciously to hide and secretly to detain', went on to warn such persons that if they did not return the books in question within forty days, they could consider themselves excommunicated. Sixtus also warned that if they were clerics, they would not be allowed to hold livings, and if laymen, they would not be allowed to hold any office at all. Also, from the date of Platina's taking up office until 1485, a register of loans from the Vatican Library was kept; and this register was headed with the warning that whoever wrote his name there in acknowledgement of books received on loan would, unless he restored them uninjured to the Pope's library within a very brief period, incur not only the Pope's anger, but his curse.

A parallel to this fifteenth century example of a librarian's curatorial function being backed up by sanctions administered by a higher authority is to be found in the legal history of nineteenth century England. Sixtus IV, with his powers of patronage and excommunication (not to mention his curse), represented the dominating influence of his time. In nineteeth century England, of course, such influence was in the hands of Parliament, and in 1861, Parliament passed an act dealing with Malicious Injuries to Property, Section 39 of which, Injuries to Works of Art, decreed: 'Whosoever shall unlawfully and maliciously destroy, or damage any Book, Manuscript . . . kept . . . in any . . . Library, or other Repository, which . . . is . . . at all Times or from Time to Time open for the Admission of the Public . . . shall be guilty of a Misdemeanor, and being convicted thereof shall be liable to be imprisoned for any Term not exceeding Six Months, with or without Hard Labour, and, if a Male under the Age of Sixteen Years, with or without Whipping'.

In the age of the printed book the real protection against the loss or decay of library materials has been the number of copies available of any given text. Even so; as Irwin points out, popular and ephemeral material still tends to disappear: and he cites in particular the fact that half the English novels issued between 1770 and 1800, which were the mainstay of the circulating libraries of that time, are no longer to be found.

William Blades, in *The enemies of books*, provides an exhaustive, if quirky, account of the various hazards to and predators of books and libraries. He notes the deleterious effects of gas and heat, for example. In the days of the last century when libraries used gas-lighting, the sulphur in the gas fumes destroyed leather bindings (especially russia leather). Heat, of course, destroys by dessication. Blades comments that books are just like children: to keep them healthy, they need an atmosphere which is pure, not too hot, not too cold, not too damp, and not too dry. He points out that dust and general neglect are destroyers also.

Blades deals at some length with the 'bookworm': which in fact appears to be a number of kinds of caterpillar and grub which feed on old wood, vegetable refuse, or fibrous material. The 'bookworm' apparently likes paper, not parchment, and therefore it is books that are attacked rather than manuscripts. Books are also attacked by other kinds of vermin—rats, for example.

Blades also deals with human predators and destroyers. His pet hatred is bookbinders who crop printed sheets or pages: who 'seem to have an ingrained antipathy to rough edges and large margins'. He likewise hates collectors who cut or tear out pages of books—especially title-pages, illuminated initials, frontispieces and plates. He is also wary of the mischiefs of servants and children.

He is consequently an admirer of those librarians and others who are capable of rescuing or salvaging books from such perils. He recounts with approbation how the books 'sadly injured' by the fire in 1862 at the Dutch Reformed Church, Austin Friars, London, were restored by 'their indefatigable librarian', by means of drying, washing, sizing, pressing and binding. A similar salvage operation—on a more massive scale—was mounted in our own times, following the disastrous flooding of Florence in November, 1966. A huge, dedicated rescue operation by hundreds of student volunteers, under the supervision of experts, saved and restored most of the inundated books and manuscripts.

2 EXTERNAL DISASTERS

Despite the depredations caused by the perishability of materials, the carelessness of users, general negligence, theft, malicious damage, atmospheric effects, bookworms, vermin, incompetent bookbinders, irresponsible book-collectors, servants and children, and despite the curatorial efforts of librarians, it remains a fact of library history that most harm to books and libraries has been caused by external disasters— whether accidental, or the result of social, political, civil or religious strife. A brief, and no more than partial, catalogue of such disasters will demonstrate this fact most clearly.

The long toll of destruction of books and libraries stretches far back into history. Writing of the pre-Christian era, John L Thornton (6) notes that in 221 BC, Shih Huang Ti, the founder of the Ch'in dynasty, ordered the destruction of all books except those on agriculture, divination and medicine; this law was not repealed until 190 BC. In Christian times, St Luke's is one of the earliest records of the wholesale destruction of books: when, after the preaching of Paul, many of the Ephesians brought out their books on 'curious arts' and burned them.

The larger part of the Alexandrian Library was consumed by fire during Caesar's Alexandrian War in 48 BC, and again burned by the Saracens in 640 AD. This final destruction was wrought by the 'ignorant and fanatical caliph', (7) Caliph Omar. 'If,' the Caliph is reported to have declared, 'these writings of the Greeks agree with the Koran, or book of Allah, they are useless, and need not be preserved; if they disagree, they are pernicious, and ought to be destroyed.'

The destruction or dispersal of almost every library in Rome and Italy in the fifth century was particularly thorough, according to Thornton. (8) The imperial library at Constantinople, founded by Constantine the Great in 330, was destroyed by fire in 477, by which time it contained almost 120,000 volumes. When Carthage was razed, some 500,000 volumes were estimated to have been burned, though Blades (9) is a little sceptical of this high figure.

During the Anglo-Saxon period in Britain, monastic libraries were constantly sacked and destroyed. In the ninth century, for example, the monasteries at Lastingham, Melrose, Tynemouth and Whitby were destroyed by the Danes. But in Britain, as was noted in the section on national libraries in the previous chapter, the greatest destruction of books and libraries took place in the reign of Henry VIII, on the dissolution of the monasteries. Thornton writes: 'The dissolution of the monasteries by Henry VIII, 1537-9, the Peasants' War in Germany, 1525, the Huguenot wars in France, between 1561 and 1589, all took heavy toll of libraries. Religious houses were suppressed, and their contents destroyed, thousands of invaluable manuscripts and printed books being burned. The accumulation of eight hundred years of intellectual life was ruthlessly swept away with the exception of the material acquired by persons with some knowledge of its value, who enhanced their private collections at little cost to themselves. In England the destruction was very thorough, every monastic and religious building being suppressed, and their contents spoiled. Certain college libraries benefited by the addition of confiscated material, but much scholarly material perished irretrievably.'

Dealing with the dispersal of the monastic libraries in England, Raymond Irwin (10) ascribes the greatest losses to the Act of 1550, which required that the few remaining libraries should be purged of what the Act defined as superstitious books. Such books were to be seized by officials in each district and surrendered to the diocesan to be burned immediately or otherwise defaced and destroyed. John Willis Clark (11) recounts that in 1549 commissioners were sent by Edward VI to Oxford and Cambridge, and these commissioners considered that it fell within their province to reform the libraries as well as those who used them. Again there was destruction of manuscripts: for example, the library of Oxford University was well stocked with manuscripts, in particular, the 600 which had been given by Humphrey, Duke of Gloucester, between 1439 and 1446—of these, only 3 now survive. N R Ker's list (12) of surviving books from the mediaeval libraries of Great Britain comprises only about 6,000 library books and service-books of religious houses, cathedrals and colleges (it excludes books belonging to the mediaeval libraries of Cambridge University and of the colleges at Oxford and Cambridge if they still remain in the modern libraries there). Ker points out that his statistics relating to various libraries have little bearing upon the actual size of any mediaeval library. 'Survival,' he says, 'has usually been a matter of chance'.

It was Irwin (13) who made the overall observation that the story of the religious aspects of libraries is wrapped up sadly in the history of heresy and persecution. The definitive example is surely the attitude of Caliph Omar, quoted in an earlier paragraph. But Irwin also cites Diocletian, the Council of Ephesus, John Wyclif, not to mention Henry VIII: only a few of a long procession of names 'concerned with the destruction of books, and the list could be extended to the present day'. William Blades also notes how precarious an existence books have had in times of religious troubles: how, in earlier times, heathens burned Christian literature, and in their turn, Christians burned heathen literature.

Acts of God in another sense—accidental destruction—have also taken their toll of books and libraries. The number of books burned in the Great Fire of London in 1666, for example, was enormous. Water as well as fire has wrought havoc. Blades mentions the thousands of books which have been lost at sea; in particular, he tells of the loss (unaccidental) of an Italian private library which, having been sold to a London bookseller, was shipped in three vessels from Venice, but one of these vessels was captured by Corsairs, and the pirates, disgusted at not finding any treasure, cast all the books into the sea.

Coming nearer our own times, Elmer D Johnson (14) tells how, during the years after 1933, while Germany was under the dictatorship of Adolph Hitler, public libraries were subjected to book purges and book burnings. Books by Jewish or Communist authors, in particular, were removed from circulation and often publicly burned. And during the second world war, in Britain alone, he notes that 'the total book loss ... including libraries, bookstores, and publishers' stocks, has been estimated at over 20,000,000 volumes'.

Finally, and very recently, there was the disastrous flood, mentioned earlier, in Florence in November 1966, when the Arno overflowed its banks and engulfed the city. Water, mud and debris poured into the basement stacks of one of Europe's richest libraries, the Biblioteca Nazionale Centrale. In all, more than 1,500,000 volumes disappeared under the tide, including centuries-old manuscripts; the total for the city exceeded 2,000,000 volumes.

3 THE ENEMIES OF BOOKS

From the foregoing it will be clear that the most powerful enemies of books are beyond the control of the curatorial function of librarians. Librarians, in the matter of conservation, can be no more than good housekeepers: they can reproduce or refurbish library materials—whether clay tablet, papyrus roll, parchment manuscript, or printed volume; they can organise and design proper accommodation and environment; and they can superintend use. But they have no power over the ultimate existence of libraries as such. Just as society creates libraries, so does it conserve them. That libraries are conserved by society is one of the clearest principles to emerge from any study of library history.

Libraries flourish in settled times. Irwin notes (15) that in a settled society there are established institutions such as monasteries, universities, colleges, schools, temples and royal palaces, all of which tend to set up libraries—especially those with a teaching function. In the earlier period of European library history, stability was provided by the Church. The systematic development of ecclesiastical libraries began with Cassiodorus and St Benedict in the sixth century; from that time onwards to the Renaissance there were no libraries in Western Europe that were not ecclesiastical in origin and purpose. In England until the eighteenth century, Irwin also observes, all institutional libraries, whether at the universities, at the newly-founded schools, at the cathedrals or in the many parish churches where small libraries were established, were in effect part of the ecclesiastical machinery. All that has happened in our own times is that the State has replaced the Church as the dominating influence. 'Heresy' has become 'deviationism', with similar consequences for the well-being of libraries. As Irwin says: 'The weapons of authority remain the same, and power is still wielded mainly by all the arts of the written and recorded word'. John L Thornton (16) affirms this in his comment that, unfortunately, 'political interference has too often resulted in the destruction, rather than construction, of libraries'.

Peace and prosperity are necessary for the maintenance and growth of libraries. War almost invariably leads to their destruction or dispersal. Economic depression, as in America in the 1930s, always results in serious reductions in book-funds. 'Libraries developed,' wrote Elmer D Johnson, (17) 'as civilizations reached their peak, and declined or were destroyed in periods of stress or conquest.'

Librarians do not seem to have grasped this principle that it is society which really conserves libraries, not themselves. Society employs them and they are only society's agents. Their curatorial function is a very important one, but it must never take precedence over or run counter to society's wishes and needs. The caricature of the librarian-dragon guarding his book-hoard is almost certainly a pejorative one.

However, a further principle which emerges from this survey—though it can only be said that the evidence is strong, rather than absolute—is that every book is of use. No librarian, nor indeed any other person, following one of these many disasters, has been recorded as having observed that even a single one of the books lost would not be missed. Assyriologists have celebrated and cherished every clay tablet which has survived from Nineveh. Scholars would delight in the discovery of any text from the Alexandrian Library. Any mediaeval book which has survived the destruction and dispersal of the English monastery libraries is prized. Any text which missed destruction by Shih Huang Ti, the Ephesians, Caliph Omar or Adolph Hitler, would now be valued.

Gabriel Naudé, it will be recalled, considered that 'there is no Book whatsoever, be it so bad or decried, but may in time be sought for by some person or other'; and this view has since rarely been contested. William Blades, with whose words this chapter began, regarded the possession of any book as 'a sacred trust'. Blades's tone may be a little pious for modern tastes, but the principle behind it is almost as well-established as any others which have revealed themselves so far.

References

1 BLADES, W: *The enemies of books*, 1902.
2 SAYCE, A M: *Assyria*, 1883.
3 THOMPSON, J W: *Ancient libraries*, 1940.
4 IRWIN, R: *The heritage of the English library*, 1964.
5 CLARK, J W: *The care of books*, 1901.
6 THORNTON, J L: *The chronology of librarianship*, 1941.
7 EDWARDS, E: *Libraries and founders of libraries*, 1865.
8 THORNTON, J L: *op cit*, 6.
9 BLADES, W: *op cit*, 1.
10 IRWIN, R: *The origins of the English library*, 1958.
11 CLARK, J W: *op cit*, 5.
12 KER, N R, *ed*: *Mediaeval libraries of Great Britain*, 2nd ed, 1964.
13 IRWIN, R: *op cit*, 4.
14 JOHNSON, E D: *History of libraries in the Western world*, 2nd ed, 1970.
15 IRWIN, R: *op cit*, 4.
16 THORNTON, J L: *op cit*, 6.
17 JOHNSON, E D: *op cit*, 14.

CHAPTER FOUR

The question of access

1 THE FIRST MILLENIUM

Public access to libraries seemingly goes right back to the seventh century BC, to the clay tablet libraries of Assyria. According to Jules Oppert, an Assyriologist of last century, Ashurbanipal had a large collection of clay tablets expressly prepared for the purpose of instruction and these were placed in the midst of his palace for public use. To this collection Edward Edwards (1) applied the rather fanciful designation 'Public library in clay'. Nevertheless, it is generally considered that Ashurbanipal's library, like the Alexandrian Library a few centuries later, was 'open to scholars, both official and unofficial'. (2)

The Alexandrian Library, of course, was specially formed by the first Ptolemy in the third century BC for the use of the scholars assembled by him at Alexandria. Demetrios of Phaleron, the first librarian of the Alexandrian Library, appears—as will have been obvious to the reader from the first section of chapter two—to have been primarily a collection-builder; but his successor, Zenodotus of Ephesus, during his incumbency (from the beginning of the reign of the second Ptolemy) made the library available for 'free public access'. (3)

Throughout Greece, by the end of the third century BC, libraries were a common feature, and Polybius, the Greek historian, 'reported that research could be carried on by any citizen in any one of Greece's major cities'. (4) Rather less reliable apparently, is the tradition that the Athenian tyrant, Peisistratus (c600-528BC) threw open his collection for public use and that the Athenians themselves added to it. However, it must be conceded that any reading of the life and achievements of Peisistratus certainly provides a good deal of circumstantial evidence to support this tradition. Peisistratus was a cultured and intelligent ruler whose policy was one of promoting the economic, cultural and artistic progress of the Athenian community. His reign is famous for its festivals, for being the period of the Attic black-figured vases, and for being the time when Athens itself became a flourishing and beautiful city. His motivation, which has been described as a 'peculiar mixture of religion, patriotism, and self-aggrandizement', (5) is very reminiscent of that of Ashurbanipal and the Ptolemies. More than that, it is commonly accepted that when Lycurgus on his travels in Ionia found that the single sections into which Homer had been broken up were being recited there, he gathered up these separate parts and brought them to Greece, 'where Peisistratus later had them put together into the *Iliad* and the *Odyssey*'. (6) It is surely not too far-fetched an inference that a man of Peisistratus's scholarly interests would have some kind of library of his own, nor that bearing in mind his general policy of cultural advancement he should have made his library available to others in Athens. Nevertheless, the comment of James Westfall Thompson (7) must be borne in mind: that in Greece, 'A reading public of any dimension assuredly is not to be thought of before the fifth century BC'; though later, 'In Athens even women and slaves were not prevented from learning to read and write'.

In Rome, we are told, the idea of a public library with large collections of volumes designed for common use first found practical realisation in the time of the first Roman emperor, Augustus. Augustus (63BC-14AD) was also a cultured man, himself the author of a number of works (none of which have survived), as well as being an administrator of genius. It was he who claimed to have found the city of Rome brick, and left it marble. He built many fine buildings—baths, theatres, temples—and two public libraries, one in connection with the Temple of Apollo on the Palatine Hill; and the Octavian Library on the Campus Martius. It is worthy of note that a constant feature of the history of libraries is that they so often owe their creation to the efforts of the most powerful figures in the overall history of mankind: Ashurbanipal, Alexander the Great, the Ptolemies and Augustus are just the first of a very long line. Libraries seem always to have been an adjunct of power.

Julius Caesar, indeed, had previously planned a public library, proposing to leave the implementation of his plans to the scholar and writer Marcus Terentius Varro. Varro, being the author of a treatise on libraries, *De bibliothecis* (which has also not survived), therefore qualifies as one of the earliest library consultants—though, of course, the very first candidate for such a title must have been Demetrios of Phaleron, library adviser to the Ptolemies at Alexandria. In the event though, Caesar was murdered (in 44BC) before his plans materialised.

The first public library in Rome was established by Gaius Asinius Pollio (76BC-4AD), a friend of Virgil and Horace, from the proceeds of the booty he obtained as a result of subduing the Parthini, an Illyrian people, in 39BC. He built the library in the Temple of Libery, Atrium Libertatis, which he restored, on the Aventine Hill. Pliny described the foundation of this library in his *Natural history*, using the phrase 'ingenia hominum rem publicam'—meaning that Asinius Pollio had made men's talents and mental powers a public possession. This phrase of course constitutes a sufficient motto for the long crusade to make libraries readily available to the entire population, and contains in a succinct form the complete justification for the principle that libraries should be for all.

Augustus's example was followed by subsequent Roman emperors. Libraries were set up by Tiberius, Vespasian, and Trajan—the latter, in particular, being responsible about

100AD for the Biblioteca Ulpia. Trajan, who ruled 98-117AD, also erected a library in Athens, above the door of which was written one of the earliest of library regulations: 'No book shall be taken out, since we have sworn an oath to that effect'. (8)

Kenyon notes also that eventually in the Roman Empire, 'Private libraries became so common that Seneca, writing in the middle of the first century, declares that a library was considered as necessary an ornament of a house as a bathroom . . . . Books were bought by the rich for show, and were numbered by thousands, even though their owners never read them. In short, in the first century of Imperial Rome private libraries were as much a necessity for an educated man as in eighteenth-century England, and public libraries were at the service of all who could read.' (9) And H L Pinner observes (10) that according to the regional census of Constantine in 350AD, there were by that time some 28 public libraries in Rome; and in the provinces too, there were collections of books, even in the smaller towns.

In any survey of public access to the libraries of the first millenium it must however be borne in mind that conditions cannot really be equated with those of our own times. For one thing, literacy was not widespread: hence Kenyon's reservation that the libraries of Rome were public only in the sense that they were at the service of those who could read. Thornton, (11) while noting that the users of the public libraries of Rome would include Greek slaves—they being among the best educated individuals—stresses also that when speaking of ancient libraries as being public, 'it is not quite in the same sense as we now consider the term. Scholars were welcomed in many libraries, both to enhance the reputations of the collections, and to secure additions. The common people were in most cases not sufficiently educated to appreciate libraries, so that if they were granted admittance to the libraries, they were unable to take advantage of the facilities provided.'

65

C Seymour Thompson agrees (12) that it is necessary for a complete history of public access to libraries that we should look 'almost to the beginning of civilisation', but he likewise points out that ancient libraries could be used only by the relatively few people who could read, and that moreover, they were accessible only within the considerable limitations 'imposed by social conditions and conventions'. In other words, it was unlikely that a galley-slave would have either the time, the opportunity or the competence to visit the Octavian Library on the Campus Martius. In the first millennium it can therefore be said that the principle that libraries are for all was severely inhibited by social and educational limitations.

2 ACCESS TO MEDIAEVAL LIBRARIES

It is the contention of John Willis Clark (13) that 'all mediaeval libraries were practically public', and that 'monastic libraries were the public libraries of the Middle Ages'. He enlarges on these statements as follows: 'I do not mean that strangers were let in, but even in those of the monasteries, books were let out on the deposit of a sufficient caution; and in Houses such as S Victor and S Germain des Près, Paris, and at the Cathedral of Rouen, the collections were open to readers on certain days of the week. The Papal library and those at Urbino and Florence were also public; and even at Oxford and Cambridge there was practically no objection to lending books on good security. Secular corporations followed the example set by the Church, and lent their manuscripts, but only on security.'

Clark then goes on to describe how these libraries were as a general rule divided into a lending library and a library of reference, the two divisions being variously christened. In the Vatican Library of Sixtus IV, there was the common library (*Bibliotheca communis*) or public library (*Bibliotheca publica*), and the reserved library (*Bibliotheca secreta*). At Santa Maria Novella, in Florence, there was the library, and the lesser library (*Bibliotheca minor*). In Cambridge University

Library, there was 'the public library', containing the more ordinary books and open to everybody, and 'the private library', containing the more valuable books and open only to a privileged few. Also in Cambridge, at Queen's College, the books which could be lent (*libri distribuendi*) were kept in a separate room from those which were chained to the shelves (*libri concatenati*); at King's College, there was a public library (*Bibliotheca magna*), and a lesser library (*Bibliotheca minor*); and as indicated by the catalogue of 1418 of Peterhouse, Cambridge, its 380 volumes were divided into books for the use of the Fellows (*libri distribuendi*) and books chained in the library (*libri cathenati in libraria*). 'In short,' Clark concludes, 'in every large collection some such division was made, either structural, or by means of a separate catalogue.' D M Norris likewise notes (14) that, in the eleventh century, in each Benedictine monastery, there were two collections of books: '(1) books that could be borrowed either by the monks, or the laymen outside the monastery, and (2) books which were kept under lock and key, and which were looked upon as part of the valuable property of the house. In other words, the Benedictines built up lending and reference collections of books.'

From the foregoing it would appear that the mediaeval definition of access was also a narrow and limited one. First of all, not only would illiteracy bar most of the population automatically, but lack of rank and status too; and even then, it seems to have been necessary to have been well-known to the institution concerned before any kind of access was permitted.

Next was the considerable hurdle of actually negotiating a loan. Kenyon (15) observes that though loans were a regular practice, 'the conditions of loans were rigidly defined, and security had to be given for each book borrowed'. Clark tells (with something approaching approval, surprisingly) of the rigmarole which ensued when Louis XI wished to borrow a certain work on medicine from the École de Médicine of Paris. The École declined to lend it until the king had deposited twelve marks worth of plate and one hundred gold crowns. The king agreed to do this, the book was borrowed and copied, and when returned to the Ecole on 24th January 1472, the king's deposit was repaid.

It must be inferred from this account of the experience of Louis XI that if a king was put to so much trouble, those of lesser rank are not likely to have fared much better. Even the brethren of a monastery were not themselves dealt with lightly in the matter of borrowing books. Lanfranc, Archbishop of Canterbury in the eleventh century, laid down in his monastic constitutions that every year, on the first Sunday of Lent, 'Before the brethren go in to chapter, the librarian should have all the books save those that were given out for reading the previous year collected on a carpet in the chapter-house; last year's books should be carried in by those who have had them, and they are to be warned by the librarian in the chapter the previous day of this. The passage from the Rule of St Benedict concerning the observance of Lent shall be read, and when a sermon has been made on this the librarian shall read out a list of the books which the brethren had the previous year. When each hears his name read out he shall return the book which was given to him to read, and anyone who is conscious that he has not read in full the book he received shall confess his fault prostrate and ask for pardon. Then the aforesaid librarian shall give to each of the brethren another book to read, and when the books have been distributed in order he shall at the same chapter write a list of the books and those who have received them.' (16)

Further, not only must the number of individuals who were able to gain access to mediaeval libraries have been extremely limited, and not only were loans strictly regulated and obtainable only against the deposit of some form of security, but even within these considerable restrictions—as Clark's account makes clear—only a proportion of a mediaeval library was 'public'. The rest was the 'private library', or the *Bibliotheca secreta*', or the *'libri cathenati in libraria'*; and of these, surely the latter is the most symbolic—the concept of a chained book, an anathema to modern eyes.

But the reasons for this jealous care of what were truly precious, rare and hard-won items have already been made plain in the second section of chapter two. Before the age of printing, every book was unique, and was produced only by dint of laborious copying. Libraries were very small, and grew at a painfully slow rate. The whole business of assembling, preserving and increasing a collection was an enormous struggle. Books were therefore naturally regarded as being very valuable.

Clark, in examining the statutes of the various early Oxford colleges, found that the 'Common Books' of the House (that is, those intended for the common use of the inmates) were placed on the same footing as the charters, muniments and valuables. They were kept in chests secured by two or three locks, and the presence of two or three officials was required for the chests to be opened. If a scholar required a book, he had to write a receipt for it. If he did not return the book, he had to pay the value of it. The whole collection was audited once a year before the Master and assembled Fellows.

Against such a background, it will be understood that access to mediaeval libraries can hardly be regarded as representing any great improvement over access to ancient libraries. A 'public' need was again recognised, but circumstances still did not permit that need to be fully met.

3 ACCESS IN MODERN TIMES

Only with the mediaeval universities, according to Johnson, (17) did there emerge libraries 'that would not only preserve the heritage of the past, but that would also open it up to general use'. He argues that 'for libraries to be a great cultural influence, they must be used; their doors must be open to large numbers of scholars and students, so that the information contained in their volumes can be disseminated to the largest possible proportion of the population'.

But judged on this argument, the library of the mediaeval university of course represents only a very modest beginning. Johnson himself describes the rules for the use of the Sorbonne

Library in the early fourteenth century: books were to be used only in the building in which the library was housed, and if taken from the library room they had to be returned before the end of the day; if anyone other than a student or a teacher took a book from the library, he had to leave a deposit of equal value; and though there was a loan collection called the great or common library, many of the books were chained.

Johnson points out that the truly public library—that is, the 'general library that is not only publicly owned but which is also in general use by any citizen who desires to use it', and more particularly, 'the municipal or regional circulating library'—does not appear on the European scene until the late nineteenth century, and in many respects is a twentieth century development.

C Seymour Thompson argues similarly, maintaining that a truly public library was not possible before the Renaissance and the Reformation. 'Slowly', he says, 'the new educational purpose and the new altruism which came from those movements directed the course of libraries into two channels, which, through the ages, have been almost imperceptibly drawing closer together. One, a channel of culture, led toward higher education and increase of knowledge; to the great libraries for scholars and the private collections of bibliophiles and men of letters. The other, originating in the church, narrow and shallow at first but gradually becoming broader and deeper, ran directly to the masses, promoting wider diffusion of knowledge.' He concludes that to 'the enriching and liberalizing streams flowing through these slowly converging channels' can be traced the origin of the modern concept of the public library.

One of the pioneers in the making of libraries public was Gabriel Naudé, whose contribution to the concept has already been mentioned, in the first chapter of this book. As Cardinal Mazarin's librarian, he travelled the length and breadth of Europe in search of valuable and splendid books, until he had gathered together the largest and most superb library of his age; but, says Edward Edwards, (18) he 'chiefly plumed himself, not upon the beauty, or the rarity, or the costliness of his collection, but on its free accessibility to all men'—on his library's motto, 'Come in, all you who desire to read, come in freely'. He was, indeed, as Edwards declares, 'a truly liberal promoter of learning', and in that capacity, 'greatly in advance of his generation'.

In the seventeenth century also, John Durie wrote *The reformed librarie-keeper* (printed 1650). John Durie (1596-1680) was a busy and much-travelled protestant divine, whose only connection with librarianship was his appointment in 1650 as library-keeper of the books, medals and manuscripts of St James's; but his view of the need that libraries should be publicly available is as advanced as that of Naudé. Durie wrote as follows: 'It is true that a fair Librarie, is not onely an ornament and credit to the place where it is; but an useful commoditie by itself to the publick; yet in effect it is no more then a dead Bodie as now it is constituted, in comparison of what it might bee, if it were animated with a publick Spirit to keep and use it, and ordered as it might bee for publick service.'

Durie also comments, with great disapproval, on a particular library: 'What a great stir hath been heretofore, about the Eminencie of the Librarie of Heidelberg, but what use was made of it? It was ingrossed into the hands of a few, till it became a Prey unto the enemies of the Truth.' It was, he declares, 'a Talent digged in the ground'.

Durie's remarks might of course also be applied to the monastic libraries of mediaeval England. They were 'ingrossed into the hands of a few', and they certainly fell 'Prey unto the enemies of the Truth'. Their wholesale destruction, unresisted by the general population, could also be considered as containing a political element: the outcome of what has since been described as 'the restiveness of the disinherited', (19) reacting against the paraphernalia and trappings of the socially and economically privileged.

Such was certainly and undeniably true of the French Revolution, in the eighteenth century. The overturn of the feudal establishment of church, state and nobility did not in this instance result in the destruction of libraries, but (as was noted in the section on national libraries in chapter two) in the reclaiming by the people of their inheritance: the confiscation from the church and the nobility of some 8,000,000 books, which were then gathered together in general book deposits in various parts of the country, with the more valuable volumes going into the Bibliothèque Nationale. And, of course, the Royal Library became the National Library.

The political factor in the movement towards public libraries was also evidenced by the Russian Revolution, in the early years of the twentieth century. The Russian people wanted peace, land, and food: and they repossessed libraries also. Again as was noted in chapter two, entire libraries were transferred to the Lenin State Library.

The other major factor, of course, was the educational factor: the spread of popular education. In countries such as France and Germany, the establishment of public educational systems began early in the nineteenth century. The United States and Britain hung on to their laissez-faire system of public education a little longer; but in the former, the common school eventually became the rule, and in the latter, with the passing in 1870 of the Elementary Education Act, there was established a system of elementary schools which were the responsibility of the state. And as Sir Frederic Kenyon has remarked, it was not until universal elementary education was established in Britain 'that the foundation was laid for the creation of a reading public coextensive with the nation'. (20)

The public library movement as such began vigorously in both Britain and in the United States in the nineteenth century, and its development in these two countries will be treated in the remaining two sections of this present chapter. But it should not be forgotten that Panizzi of the British Museum Library was one of the foremost advocates of the principle that libraries should be available to all. Edward Miller (21) not only quotes the sentence at the heart of Panizzi's evidence in 1836 before the Select Committee on the British Museum—'I want a poor student to have the same means of indulging his learned curiosity, of following his rational pursuits, of consulting the same authorities, of fathoming the most intricate inquiry as the richest man in the kingdom, as far as books go, and I contend that the Government is bound to give him the most liberal and unlimited assistance in this respect'—but also comments: 'here is the essential radicalism of the man, his proud assertion, in *laissez-faire* and caste-ridden England, of the fundamental rights of any student, however poor and humble, to have the very best available and the obligation, nay, the duty, of the state to provide it, whatever the cost. This sentiment, which we in the twentieth century take so much for granted, was [then] new and revolutionary.' And it was Panizzi who, after Thomas Carlyle had complained that as an eminent historian he had not received suitably preferential treatment in the famous Reading Room, declared roundly that: 'All are equal there'. It should also be recalled, as was likewise mentioned in chapter one, that Panizzi's view was notably reaffirmed in the twentieth century by Archibald MacLeish, Librarian of Congress from 1939 to 1944, when he welcomed the use of that library by 'the general public—all comers from all places'. (22)

In conclusion, mention must be made of the development of the concept of open access. Kenyon (23) having made the general comment that 'too great restriction may lead to a book spending most of its time unused on the shelves, instead of being honourably worn to pieces in the hands of readers', goes on to say: 'A vital feature of an efficient Public Library is the principle of Open Access. In the early days of public libraries the idea of allowing the general public free access to the bookshelves would have been incredible. Applicants had to choose their books from catalogues and have them handed out over a counter, as in a subscription lending library. Progressive librarians, however, early came to realise the educational

73

advantage of allowing readers to browse among the shelves and make their own selection, and the system of open access is now widely adopted and almost universally so in new buildings.'

Kenyon was writing in 1930, and it is obvious that even at that time, there was some novelty in the notion that the general public should be allowed to go to the bookshelves themselves. Open access was essentially a twentieth century development, and a particular contribution of the American library movement. More than anything else, it marks the fulfilment of the principle of free access to the contents of libraries by all: the symbolic snapping of the links of the chained book.

4 BRITISH PUBLIC LIBRARIES

Early in the eighteenth century, in the reign of Queen Anne— so Edward Edwards tells us (24)—an act was passed 'for the better preservation of Parochial Libraries', but it was only, in his words, for the purpose of 'preserving parsonic heir-looms'. Not until another hundred and fifty years had passed was there enacted legislation which effectively provided free libraries for the general British public.

There were forerunners in Britain of the public libraries, of course. The eighteenth century as such was characterised by a great enthusiasm for subscription and circulating libraries and reading societies. The largest of these did not emerge until the mid-nineteenth century, when in 1842 Edward Mudie founded his famous circulating library. There were also proprietary libraries, providing a scholarly reference and lending collection for their members: the most notable being the London Library, founded in 1841 by William Ewart Gladstone, Thomas Carlyle and others. Nor were such libraries entirely overtaken by the development of a public library system in Britain; the London Library is still in existence, and popular circulating libraries survived in numbers until the second world war.

An equally important forerunner was the mechanics' institute. Mechanics' institutes were an early form of adult

74

education in Britain: voluntary associations of mechanics and working-men which provided classes, lectures, reading-rooms and libraries. Members paid an annual subscription, and organised the running of the institutes themselves. The heyday of the mechanics' institutes was from about 1800 to about 1850.

As evidenced by the strong public interest in self-help libraries—whether subscription libraries or libraries attached to organisations such as the mechanics' institutes—the early nineteenth century was a time ripe for the greater public provision of library facilities. In Britain, as Kelly (25) observes, the impetus came from above, from the ruling class, rather than because of revolutionary agitation from below. Kelly quotes a letter from Charles Henry Bellenden Ker to Lord Brougham, dated 1831, making the first precise proposal for a rate-aided public library service that is known. However, it was Edward Edwards, in tandem with William Ewart, who in the event brought about the establishment of public libraries in Britain.

Edwards's motivation was the improvement and education of the general populace; his political inclinations were radical, and strong. William Ewart (1798-1869), an MP described by the *Dictionary of national biography* as 'an advanced liberal', was notable not only for his advocacy of free public libraries, but also for his opposition to capital punishment. In their joint effort to establish free public libraries, Ewart planned the general strategy, and Edwards supplied the detailed material.

On 10th April 1848 (as mentioned earlier, in chapter one), Edwards published his *Remarks on the paucity of libraries freely open to the public, in the British Empire; together with a succinct statistical view of the existing provision of Public Libraries in the several states of Europe*, in the form of a letter addressed to the Earl of Ellesmere, the Chairman of the Royal Commission on the British Museum, using materials he had collected for an article in the *British quarterly review* and a paper he had delivered to the Statistical Society. Ewart wrote to him subsequently, telling Edwards of his intention

75

to press for free municipal libraries, and soliciting his help in gathering supportive evidence.

In 1849, the setting up of a Select Committee 'on the best means of extending the establishment of Libraries freely open to the Public especially in large towns in Great Britain and Ireland' was agreed by Parliament. Edwards appeared as the first witness. His aim, and that of Ewart, was to demonstrate that existing public library facilities in Great Britain were totally inadequate, and that facilities in other countries were much better. And as Kelly remarks, 'where the evidence did not support this view, Ewart was reluctant to accept it'. There were indeed, as W A Munford (26) also notes, a number of critics of the accuracy of Edwards's statistical evidence to the Select Committee.

The Committee's objective was (in Kelly's words) to obtain 'an extension of the Museums Act of 1845 to enable municipal authorities to levy a small rate for the establishment and maintenance of a library'; they believed optimistically that there was no need to subsidise the provision of books, which they thought would be supplied by donations. The Select Committee in its report duly recommended that 'a power be given by Parliament enabling Town Councils to levy a small rate for the creation and support of Town Libraries'.

On the basis of this recommendation, the Public Libraries Act of 1850 came into being, empowering municipal authorities with a population of 10,000 or more to spend a halfpenny rate on the provision of accommodation for a museum and/or library, and on the upkeep of such accommodation; but the Act did not permit any expenditure on books or specimens. There was considerable Tory opposition to the Bill, and their arguments included the view that public libraries might give rise to 'unhealthy agitation'.

Fifteen years later, in his book *Libraries and founders of libraries* (1865), Edwards wrote triumphantly that the public libraries established as a result of the Act 'are unconnected with any sort of sectarian influence, or of class distinction. There is nothing of almsgiving in their establishment;—nothing of clap-trap oratory, or of money-seeking expedients, in their means of continued support; —nothing of restriction or exaction in their terms of accessibility. They are not the Libraries of working-people; or of poor people; or of trades-people; but the Libraries of THE CITY, THE TOWN, or THE PARISH, in which they are placed. They are not only FREE, but PERMANENT. They will never become "schools of political agitation" (as one of the opponents of the first "Libraries Bill" asserted, in the House of Commons, that they would become), but, if they can be said to have any conceivable political tendency at all, it must needs be a "Conservative" one, since they plainly widen that public domain in which all classes have a common interest. Whilst essentially independent of gifts, they have been liberally, even munificently, promoted by liberal men. And they are, as yet, but at the threshold of their public usefulness.'

Kelly records that the first modern rate-aided libraries were Canterbury (1847), Warrington (1848) and Salford (1850), and he goes on to observe that the development of public libraries in Britain, from these humble beginnings until the Public Libraries Act of 1919 (which marked both the end of the penny rate and the establishment of the country library service), is a continuum without any single outstanding event. There was however from around 1887, the year of Queen Victoria's Jubilee, an increased annual rate of new libraries: prior to that time, about three or four new libraries were opened each year; subsequently, until 1900, about sixteen or seventeen a year.

One major debate, though, in this steady development was over the matter of open access, referred to in the previous section of the present chapter. While Edward Edwards dedicated his professional life to bringing about public access to libraries he was nevertheless, it is curious to note, not willing to allow the public direct access to the shelves. In this view, he was no different from other public librarians of his time; and in his published suggestions for the physical arrangement of public libraries, he recommended that the reading room or

77

rooms should be quite separate from the rooms in which the books were kept. Hence there grew up the trying system of 'indirect access'—that is, readers looked up in the library's catalogue which books they wanted, and an assistant fetched them. To save fruitless requests and searches for books which were already out on loan, the 'indicator' system was invented: a wooden frame with rows of small slots or pigeon holes, each of which represented a book, so that whether or not a book was out could be seen by users at a glance.

Kelly therefore characterises the closing years of the nineteenth century as the period which 'saw the beginning of two closely related revolutions in library practice—the open access revolution and the Dewey decimal revolution'. He records that a measure of open access to reference works was introduced at Cambridge and elsewhere as early as the 1870s. This practice gradually extended as the years went by, on the whole with great success, though of course some thefts did occur. It was however not until 1892 that James Duff Brown, the first librarian of Clerkenwell, put forward detailed proposals for 'safeguarded open access' in public lending libraries. Under this system, a reader entered the library through a controlled wicket-gate, selected his own book, and then made his exit through another wicket where his loan was recorded.

In May 1894, Brown launched his library at Clerkenwell on this principle. His opponents offered all sorts of objections, the principal of which were the likelihood of extensive thefts, disorder and misplacements among the books, increased wear and tear on the books, crowding and rowdyism among the borrowers, the reduction of storage space for books, and the fact that the system would be practically useless to a large majority of borrowers because they knew nothing about books.

Now it must be said that not one of these objections is unreasonable. Any modern librarian witnesses daily evidence of their validity: some books are stolen; books are frequently returned by readers to the wrong place on the shelves; books do get worn out more quickly in a browsing library; libraries which are heavily used by the public do have the turmoil of bus stations rather than the quiet of places of study; large crowds of readers do necessarily reduce the amount of floor area for the accommodation of actual books; and the mono-lithic mysteries of very large libraries do frequently utterly confuse and confound ordinary members of the population. But all of these objections together are still far outweighed by the advantage of free and unhindered access to collections of books; and the historical evidence which supports this view lies, if in nothing else, in the present century's recorded statistics of enormous borrowings from public lending libraries. Looked at in real terms, the picture of crowded libraries and much-wanted books makes its own incontrovertible case for open access.

James Duff Brown himself, of all the objections offered, would only concede lack of space as a valid one. Neverthe-less, Kelly is able to quote Berwick Sayers to the effect that ninety per cent of the library profession were actively anta-gonistic to open access in Brown's time. But in 1899, twelve libraries which had adopted the open access system published a pamphlet rebutting in detail the various arguments com-monly raised against open access. On the question of theft, for example, they were able to show that only one book was lost for each 27,547 books issued.

In the twentieth century in Britain, open access has become the rule, the established tradition. The same is true of the United States, and indeed of those libraries throughout the world which have been influenced by Anglo-American library practices.

The most recent landmark in the steady development of the public library system in Britain was the Public Libraries Act of 1964. With this Act, as Kelly says, 'the Central Government for the first time assumed responsibility for the supervision of the library service'. And by the late 1960s, according to Johnson, (27) nearly thirty per cent of the population of Britain were registered library users, 'making Great Britain one of the most library-conscious nations in the world'.

5 AMERICAN PUBLIC LIBRARIES

In 1848 the city of Boston was empowered by law to establish and maintain a public library: and if there was a starting-point in the development of the modern public library in America, this, the first major example in America of a tax-supported free library, may be regarded as being such.

However, as in Britain, there were many forerunners of the public library. Even in Boston itself, in the seventeenth century, the will of Robert Keayne (who died in 1656) stipulated that a room in a house was to be provided for a public library; and as a nucleus for that library, he gave his books and some 'writings' of his own. Also in the seventeenth century, Thomas Bray, appointed in 1696 as commissary for the province of Maryland, set out to provide libraries for the use of the populace. Bray was a country rector when the Bishop of London chose him to provide ecclesiastical assistance in the colony. He lived in Maryland only during part of 1700, and did most of his work from England, in correspondence with the colony. The libraries he established were meant principally for Anglican clergy, but their scope was extended. By 1699, there were 30 such libraries in Maryland and the other colonies. Bray also organised in 1698-9 the Society for Promoting Christian Knowledge, to support the libraries.

Thomas Bray stands out in the history of American libraries because of his dedication to the principle that books and libraries are to be used: in his own words—'And whereas it may be objected, that the Books will be so often Borrow'd, that it will be hard for any one to have the Book he wants. I am so far from being much concern'd to answer it, that I heartily wish the great Use and frequently Borrowing of Books out of these Libraries, may make it a real Objection.'

In the eighteenth century, in 1731, Benjamin Franklin set up a 'social library' in Philadelphia. By 1820, more than 750 such libraries had been established in towns throughout America. The social library—formed by subscribers putting an agreed sum of money into a joint stock for the purchase of books, and each subscriber paying an annual sum subsequently for the library's maintenance and increase—was practically the only agency attempting to meet the popular desire for books for nearly a century.

Subsequently, there were also the 'Athenaeums' in the various towns of America: for example, the Boston Athenaeum, founded in 1807. The 'Athenaeums' provided, for a few dollars a year, access to books and periodicals; but, as C Seymour Thompson observes, (28) though they were democratic in purpose, this kind of proprietary library was in reality democratic only in small and homogeneous communities where wealth was not unevenly distributed and social distinctions were slight. As American society grew more complex in the course of the first half of the nineteenth century, these libraries began to appear to be the preserve of what almost seemed a kind of aristocracy.

Thus the period from about 1820 to 1850 was the time when considerable efforts were being made to make the provision of libraries more abundant. One further manifestation of such efforts was the development during that period of libraries for apprentices and mechanics; libraries ('mercantile libraries') for young men pursuing a mercantile or commercial career; and 'young men's associations' which provided libraries for their members.

Next came the idea of providing small libraries attached to the common schools. This idea of an extensive system of libraries maintained by school districts under the supervision of the state is credited mainly to James Wadsworth (1768-1844), a prosperous landowner whose chief interest, apart from his business, was public education. District libraries eventually became required by law, but for a variety of reasons—the administrative unit was too small; the money made available was seldom sufficient; and their administration tended to be in the hands of untrained and inexperienced people—they never became in general as effective as had been hoped.

By the beginning of the 1850s, though, a number of public libraries had been established in towns. By the time of the

81

formation of the American Library Association in 1876, although sixteen states had passed legislation authorising the maintenance of libraries by cities and towns, among the cities of more than one hundred thousand a free public circulating library had been established in only six: Boston in 1852, Detroit in 1865, Cincinnati in 1867, Cleveland in 1868, Louisville in 1871, and Chicago in 1872.

C Seymour Thompson characterises the development of the American public library in the following terms: 'In the free public library, which now began to take a prominent place among American social institutions, we do not see a curious phenomenon, originating in the nineteenth century. We see, rather, that century's expression of ideas and objectives which had come to it, through two channels, from remote sources; an expression made ever more clear and more effective through larger concepts of needs and better perception of opportunities.

'Belief that universal education is essential for the welfare of the republic; belief in the power of books as a deterrent from vice and a source of education and culture; all this had entered into formation of social libraries, apprentices' and mercantile and young men's libraries, and school-district libraries. To this had been added a slowly growing conviction that only a free library could meet the needs of modern society; a library which should ignore the distinctions of class which had long retarded a sense of community solidarity and had left the intellectual wants of many to the mercy of charity; a library offering equal privileges to all the residents of the community maintaining it.

'Experience taught that this library could not be successfully imposed upon the people by authority. "For such an institution to accomplish its whole purpose", said the citizens' committee in Boston in 1841, "it must be in the highest sense popular. That is, it must have directly engaged in its formation and use the whole people. ... If such work is to be done all are to come to it as having an equal or a common interest in it. ... This institution can only exist through the enthusiasm of the people, and it can be created by that in a moment."

'The American public library can have no better characterization than the words graven on the present home of the Public Library of the City of Boston: "Built by the people and dedicated to the advancement of learning".'

Arthur E Bostwick, (29) another historian of the American public library, views the development of the public library in that country as being not only important in American terms, but in a universal context also. Bostwick argues that America's main contribution was not merely the great impetus that was given there to 'the idea of a collection of books for the use of an entire community, supported by that community from the proceeds of tax', but essentially the 'modern library idea': that is, features such as 'freedom of access to shelves, work with children, cooperation with schools, branch libraries, traveling libraries, and so-called "library advertising"—the effort to make the library and its work known in the community and to induce people to use it'. He adds that such modern library ideas owe their success to the fact that 'their advocates have been active men; those who dislike them are passive.'

Bostwick states that Cleveland Public Library seems to have been the first in which open access was introduced on a really large scale, the plan being introduced at the beginning of April, 1890. The first children's library he records was established in New York City in 1885 on the initiative of Emily S Hanaway; this particular development in American public librarianship grew strongly from that time, the first discussion of work with children taking place at the American Library Association conference in Philadelphia in 1897, when most of the arguments were to do with the relative merits of separate children's libraries and children's rooms.

Bostwick notes that in America, libraries' relationship with schools existed from the earliest days of libraries, with the common situation of early library collections actually being located in school buildings. More formal cooperation (for example, library deposits of books for children in school) dates from the late 1870s.

As for branch libraries, he says that the first free public branch library in the United States was the East Boston Branch of the Boston Public Library, opened in 1870; though he also records that by then, branch libraries were already operating successfully in England. Similarly with travelling libraries: the State of New York sent out its first travelling library in 1893, and this innovation spread throughout America from that time—but such libraries had existed in Scotland as early as 1810.

Nevertheless it is an historical fact that the 'modern library idea' did indeed achieve its full vigour and stature in American hands; and by the early twentieth century, had come an immense distance from—in the words of Elmer D Johnson (30)— 'the colonial tradition of opening the library only a few hours a week, with close restrictions on the use of books'.

References

1 EDWARDS, E: *Libraries and founders of libraries*, 1865.

2 JOHNSON, E D: *History of libraries in the Western world*, 2nd ed, 1970.

3 PARSONS, E A: *The Alexandrian Library*, 1952.

4 JOHNSON, E D: *op cit*, 2.

5 EHRENBERG, V: *From Solon to Socrates*, 1968.

6 BURCKHARDT, J: *History of Greek culture*, 1963.

7 THOMPSON, J W: *Ancient libraries*, 1940.

8 Quoted in THORNTON, J L: *The chronology of librarianship*, 1941.

9 KENYON, Sir F: *Libraries and museums*, 1930.

10 PINNER, H L: *The world of books in classical antiquity*, 1958.

11 THORNTON, J L: *op cit*, 8.

12 THOMPSON, C S: *Evolution of the American public library*, 1653-1876, 1952.

13 CLARK, J W: *The care of books*, 1901.

14 NORRIS, D M: *A history of cataloguing*, 1939.

15 KENYON, *Sir* F: *op cit*, 9.

16 LANFRANC, *Archbishop of Canterbury: The monastic constitutions*, trans by D Knowles, 1951.

17 JOHNSON, E D: *op cit*, 2.

18 EDWARDS, E: *Memoirs of libraries*, 1859.

19 BAINTON, R H: article on Reformation in *Encyclopaedia Britannica*, 15th ed, 1974.

20 KENYON, *Sir* F: *op cit*, 9.

21 MILLER, E: *Prince of librarians*, 1967.

22 Quoted in GOODRUM, C A: *The Library of Congress*, 1974.

23 KENYON, *Sir* F: *op cit*, 9.

24 EDWARDS, E: *op cit*, 1.

25 KELLY, T: *A history of public libraries in Great Britain, 1845-1965,* 1973.

26 MUNFORD, W A: *Edward Edwards*, 1963.

27 JOHNSON, E D: *op cit*, 2.

28 THOMPSON, C S: *op cit*, 12.

29 BOSTWICK, A E: *The American public library*, 1910.

30 JOHNSON, E D: *op cit*, 2.

CHAPTER FIVE

The purposes of libraries

1 LIBRARIES AS STOREHOUSES OF KNOWLEDGE

When he founded his library at Nineveh, Ashurbanipal invoked the aid of his favourite god, Nebo. 'I have collected these tablets,' he wrote, 'I have had them copied, I have marked them with my name, and I have deposited them in my palace.' (1) Nebo (or Nabu) was the deity of wisdom and the teacher of agriculture and letters, whose emblems included a measuring rod, a stylus and a writing tablet; in Hebrew mythology, Nebo appeared as the keeper of the tablets of fate. Ashurbanipal was consciously creating a storehouse of religious, historical, geographical, legal and scientific knowledge from all parts of the known world; and he intended this storehouse to be of use to his subjects.

The Alexandrian library was, similarly, a universal storehouse of knowledge, containing as it eventually did almost all of the extant literature. Such was the declared and recorded aim of its first librarian, Demetrios of Phaleron. And again. as at Nineveh, the Alexandrian storehouse was not created only to preserve knowledge, but to disseminate it: hence the assembly by the Ptolemies of a great body of scholars to work on the materials gathered there.

With Nineveh and Alexandria was established the principle that libraries are for the storage and dissemination of knowledge. The principle was maintained, however dimly, throughout the Middle Ages, though the emphasis then tended to be on preservation rather than dissemination. In mediaeval times it was felt that no monastery or convent could be without books, and John Willis Clark (2) quotes an appropriate epigram from 1170: 'claustrum sine armario, castrum sine armamentario' (a monastery without a library is like a castle without an armoury).

In our own times, the principle of both storage and dissemination flourishes strongly. The Library of Congress contains virtually all of man's recorded knowledge, and that knowledge is available to all. The British Museum Library in the mid-eighteenth century opened its great store of knowledge to the world, and since then the world has been further enriched as a consequence, by the fruits of the talents and labours of those who were thus able to make use of that knowledge. Robert Cowtan in his *Memories of the British Museum* (3) recalls that in the days of the Montague Place Reading-Rooms, those who read there included Wordsworth, Southey, Sir Walter Scott, Charles Lamb, Coleridge, Washington Irving, Sydney Smith, Henry Hallam, Macaulay, Thackeray and Dickens. In later times, the names have been just as illustrious. Karl Marx, the founder of modern communist doctrine, who lived in London from 1849 until the end of his life, acquired in the British Museum Library his deep knowledge of economics and of the economic development of Europe; and this knowledge bore fruit in his famous work, *Das Kapital* (1867). George Bernard Shaw, the playwright, as a young man completed his education in the Reading Room of the British Museum, spending all his afternoons there reading and writing. And in addition to these more famous names, of course, are the tens of thousands of lesser-known scholars who have over the years based their researches on the collections of the British Museum Library, and so both disseminated and increased the knowledge to be found there.

For more than twenty-five hundred years libraries have had a virtual monopoly on the storage of human knowledge. A library is the only human institution to which an individual can turn for a permanent and comprehensive store of information. Fremont Rider, it will be recalled from chapter two, referred to the great libraries as 'the stored-up knowledge of the race', 'the building blocks of civilization'. And Thomas Carlyle expressed it thus: (4) 'In Books lies the *soul* of the whole Past Time; the articulate audible voice of the Past, when the body and material substance of it has altogether vanished like a dream. Mighty fleets and armies, harbours and arsenals, vast cities, high-domed, many-engined,—they are precious, great: but what do they become? Agamemnon, the many Agamemnons, Pericleses, and their Greece; all is gone now to some ruined fragments, dumb mournful wrecks and blocks: but in the Books of Greece! There Greece, to every thinker, still very literally lives; can be called up again into life. No magic *Rune* is stranger than a Book. All that mankind has done, thought, gained or been: it is lying as in magic preservation in the pages of Books.'

The principle that one of the purposes of a library is to store knowledge has never been contested. Any other purposes of a library are ancillary, and relate to the use made of that knowledge. It is an inevitable kind of logic that a library cannot remain only a store, for what it contains is valueless if it is not disseminated. It must be concluded therefore that the principle which has been established over the past twenty-five centuries is a double-barrelled one—that libraries are for the storage *and* the dissemination of knowledge—and the remainder of this chapter will be concerned with some of the real or supposed effects of that dissemination.

2 MORAL AND POLITICAL ASPECTS

There is no evidence whatsoever that the founders of the Alexandrian Library looked for some moral effects to result from its establishment. There was indeed a political purpose, in that the Library glorified the culture of Greece and therefore increased patriotism and nationalistic feeling. Ashurbanipal, on the other hand, must have been aware of the moral, social and political effects of disseminating knowledge by means of a library, because he apparently exercised a strict censorship. Johnson records (5) that one of Ashurbanipal's scribe-librarians is reported to have said of the library: 'I shall place in it whatever is agreeable to the king; what is not agreeable to the king, I shall remove from it'.

The control of libraries for the purposes of propaganda, of course, has been a recurrent feature of library history over its entire span. Mention has already been made, in chapter 3, of control for religious reasons: Caliph Omar destroying all books which did not agree with the teachings of the Koran, and Henry VIII's destruction in England of monastic libraries, to quote but two examples. In relation to our own times, in the matter of political control, Johnson reminds us that in Nazi Germany libraries were made a part of the propaganda system, and all efforts were directed toward the development of a strong German nationalism.

The earliest reference to the moral effect of libraries is the inscription written over the door of the library established at Thebes by the great king of Egypt, Rameses II (c1304-c1237BC)—the king celebrated by Shelley in his poem *Ozymandias* ('Two vast and trunkless legs of stone / Stand in the desert . . . Near them, on the sand, / Half sunk, a shattered visage lies, whose frown, / And wrinkled lip, and sneer of cold command, / Tell that its sculptor well those passions read'). Incidentally, though the achievements of Rameses II (or Ozymandias) may have been over-glorified by ancient writers, he nevertheless appears to have been another prime example of an extraordinarily powerful figure with a significant place in library history. The inscription above the door of his library has been variously translated as 'The soul's dispensary' (Edward Edwards), or 'Medicine for the soul' (James Westfall Thompson), or 'The hospital of the soul' (Kenyon): but the drift is plain enough.

In the Middle Ages, of course, all monastic and religious libraries were expressly for the greater honour and glory of God. It will be recalled by the reader that the monastic constitutions laid down by Lanfranc required that each of the

brethren should read at least one book a year, and that therefore 'anyone who is conscious that he has not read in full the
book he received shall confess his fault prostrate and ask for
pardon'.

However, it was in the nineteenth century, when the demand for greater provision of libraries available to the general
public became strongest, that most thought was given to the
possible effects—moral, social and political—of such provision.
Early in the debates which attended the passage of the 1850
Public Libraries and Museums Bill through the House of
Commons, one Member, Mr Brotherton, referred to the
'immense moral good' which would result from their establishment. On the other hand, one of the Bill's most vehement
critics, Colonel Sibthorp, described libraries merely as institutions providing 'amusements and recreation', and he added
that he supposed Parliament would soon be 'thinking of
supplying the working classes with quoits, peg-tops, and foot-
ball'. A supporter of the Bill, Mr Hume, thought however
that 'it was much better that the people should have the opportunity of spending their time in public libraries in preference to public houses'. And another MP, Mr Wyld, hinted
that some of the opposition to the Bill was from 'the agri-
cultural interest', since the establishment of public libraries
would lead to the diminished consumption of an article in
which they largely dealt (malt): 'because it appeared, from
the whole course of evidence on this subject, that, in proportion as institutions of this kind were established, drunken-
ness and crime had diminished'.

Thomas Kelly (6) notes that James Silk Buckingham
(1786-1855) was a good example of those early nineteenth
century members of Parliament who advocated free public
libraries to distract the labouring classes from their prevalent
vices—principally, intoxication. Kelly also refers to what he
calls 'the most famous cartoon in English library history',
designed by J Williams Benn, and reproduced as the frontis-
piece to the first edition of Thomas Greenwood's *Free public
libraries* (1866). This cartoon shows the two 'rivals'—on the

one side, the Free Library, and on the other, the Red Lion pub and a bagatelle and billiards room. Linked with the idea of providing libraries and museums was the idea of providing public walks and gardens, or open spaces for athletic and healthy exercises: all to counteract vice.

Edward Edwards, it will be recalled from the previous chapter, always denied that free public libraries would become, as had been asserted in some quarters, 'schools of political agitation', but he did believe (7) that every step taken to extend the usefulness of a library, to diffuse far and wide the best thoughts of the best thinkers, would put one more mine beneath 'the social abuses which have so often placed a prevailing influence over our public institutions within the grasp of cunning money-grubs, or of noisy stump-orators'. Indeed, as Kelly observes, the original impetus for public libraries came from philanthropists and reformers, who saw them as an ameliorating influence; and it was not until later in the nineteenth century that the connection of libraries with social reform diminished.

However, even as late as 1891, Kelly quotes Greenwood as still arguing in favour of public libraries on the basis that it is want of amusement that drives men to vice and crime—though he also remained troubled by the conviction that libraries are socialistic institutions and nurseries of socialism. Kelly also quotes from the arguments offered by a committee at Willesden in 1891 organising the campaign for a public library there: 'They furnish a place of safe and healthful resort to young people and they develop intelligence, sobriety and self-respect in both young and old'. He cites too, the belief of Sir John Lubbock, expressed in 1890, that a 'great part . . . of what we spend on books we save in prisons and police'; and he caps all this by quoting from a hymn composed especially for the opening in 1887 of the Fielden Public Library in Fleetwood, Lancashire, which praises the benefactors

'Who nobly make provision
To feed the hungry mind,
Who use their wealth and influence,

And throw a cheering ray
To lighten life's rough journey
And cheer man on his way.'

In his history of the evolution of the American public library, C Seymour Thompson records (8) that Thomas Bray, appointed in 1696 as commissary for the province of Marynand, considered that, in respect of the 'younger gentry' in England, libraries would 'ennoble their Minds with Principles of Vertue and true Honour', and 'file off that Roughness, Ferity and Barbarity, which are the never failing fruits of Ignorance and Illiterature'.

In the eighteenth century in America, Benjamin Franklin set up his Philadelphia 'social library' with the primary purpose of self-education; but such libraries (in the words of the catalogue printed in 1766 of the Juliana Library of Lancaster, Pa) were also to inspire 'a Love of Freedom, and an Abhorrence of Slavery', showing to all 'the true Value of Liberty, and how great a Price the Preservation thereof has cost our Forefathers'. Franklin himself was aware of a political motive, believing that such libraries contributed in some degree to the stand made throughout the colonies in defence of their privileges. They also promoted, C Seymour Thompson observes, the American citizen's desire for equality, because it was thought possible to achieve that equality by a general diffusion of knowledge, and to obtain equality of privilege, opportunity and achievement, by learning. As Thomas Jefferson wrote in 1809: 'The people of every country are the only safe guardians of their own rights, and are the only instruments which can be used for their destruction. And certainly they would never consent to be so used were they not deceived. To avoid this, they should be instructed to a certain degree. I have often thought that nothing would do more extensive good at small expense than the establishment of a small circulating library in every country, to consist of a few well-chosen books, to be lent to the people of the country, under such regulations as would secure

92

their safe return in due time. These should be such as would give them a general view of other history, and particular view of that of their own country, a tolerable knowledge of Geography, the elements of Natural Philosophy, of Agriculture and Mechanics.'

Americans also thought that their intellectual independence was following their political independence far too slowly. They felt the need to stimulate an indigenous culture and learning. It was this feeling which led to the establishment in 1807 of the Boston Athenaeum, providing a reading room containing the principal European and American periodical publications, and a library. Such 'Athenaeums' subsequently spread throughout the country. The idea was to provide an agreeable place of resort, accessible during most hours, which provided opportunities for literary intercourse and for reading literary and miscellaneous literature, the whole being a centre of learning and culture, the establishment of which demonstrated not only a love of these, but also patriotism and public spirit. The privileges of such places were available for a few dollars a year. The Boston Athenaeum described itself as 'a fountain, at which all, who choose, may gratify their thirst for knowledge'. The Providence Athenaeum also described itself as a fountain, 'a fountain of living water, at which the intellectual thirst of the whole community may be slaked'.

Again, in view of the supposed moral benefits of libraries, William Wood, a Boston merchant, set out from 1819 to set up libraries for mechanics and apprentices—first in Boston, and then in New York, Albany, Philadelphia and New Orleans. 'To draw them [the mechanics and apprentices] from scenes of idleness and vice', he wrote, 'it is proposed to form a Library of suitable Books'. Both the 'social libraries' and these apprentices' libraries, says C Seymour Thompson, shared the aim of 'moral betterment'. And during the period of movement towards a system of libraries attached to common schools, Superintendent Spencer in New York in 1839 acclaimed the school district library as 'the solace of age, the guide of youth, the stay of manhood, the source of so much happiness to parents and their children'.

This moral view persisted well into the era of tax-supported free public libraries. In 1847, in Boston, a committee of the City Council was appointed to consider the foundation of a library, and when it reported in favour of the proposal it advanced as one of its arguments that a public library would 'by supplying an innocent and praiseworthy occupation prevent a resort to those scenes of amusement that are prejudicial to the elevation of the mind'.

3 LIBRARIES FOR EDUCATION

When, in 1850 in the House of Commons, William Ewart moved for leave to bring in a Bill to enable town councils to establish public libraries, he used their educational value as one of his main arguments: 'There were two kinds of education', he told Parliament 'that imparted in schools, and that acquired by individuals themselves; and they had the authority of Gibbon for saying that the education which a man gave to himself was far more important than that which he could acquire from a teacher. In public libraries the opportunity of self-teaching would be afforded to the labouring classes. The Americans had made far greater advancement in the matter than the people of this country had. In every state of the Union there was a library kept up by the State, and accessible to the public, and from them the people derived immense benefit. There was scarcely a native of the United States who could not read.'

Edward Edwards maintained a more specific and more restrictive view than Ewart's, while in no way denying the connection of libraries with education. 'National libraries,' he wrote, 'should be the store-houses whence educators of every kind may derive their materials, rather than direct educational agents themselves'. Panizzi did not doubt the educational purpose of libraries, but he was not sure that the general population took the same view. In his evidence to the Select Committee on the British Museum in 1836, he

94

said: (10) 'As to its most important and most noble purpose as an establishment for the furtherance of education for study and research, the public seem to be, almost, indifferent'.

Ewart's reference to the enthusiasm in America for the provision of libraries as one of the means of public education is certainly borne out by C Seymour Thompson's history of the evolution of the American public library. In his introduction, Thompson defines 'the modern library movement' in the United States as follows: 'By this term is meant the development of the library as an agency for popular education, untrammelled by traditions and restraints of earlier times and inspired to activities far beyond all former vision'.

It will be recalled from the previous section of this chapter that the 'social library' which Benjamin Franklin set up in Philadelphia in 1731 was essentially, in Thompson's view, for the purpose of self-education. Democracy could only be won and maintained, it was believed, through democracy of education and education for democracy. As Richard Beresford wrote in 1797: 'The best means by which to perpetuate the liberty we may yet be said to hold, is the information of the whole mass of the people'. Thompson also characterises the 'social library' as 'a manifestation of earnest desire for education, the gateway to equality and to success'; and in explanation of the great impetus in America for free libraries, he writes: 'That universal education is essential in a democracy was a truism; and until theory could be translated into fact our political and social structure was insecure'. Thompson has already been quoted, in the previous section of this chapter, as noting that both the 'social libraries' and the apprentices' libraries shared the aim of moral betterment; but he adds also that the other aims were 'intellectual improvement, and what we now call adult education'.

Thompson stresses the point that the cornerstone of American education was the conviction, 'born of the Reformation and nourished by the revolution', that universal education is essential for religious, political, and intellectual freedom. And in retailing the arguments put forward by the

95

committee set up by the City Council of Boston in 1847 to discuss the foundation of a free library—one of which was 'It will give to the young when leaving school an opportunity to make further advances in learning and knowledge'—he observes that these and other considerations 'foreshadowed the coming of a library of broader educational purpose, where both the general reader and the serious student would find his wants supplied'.

In England, it was not until after the Education Act of 1870, which accepted the principle of universal elementary education, that libraries began to be linked with the great surge forward of national education; and it was philanthropists and reformers who saw in them an ameliorating and educational force: public libraries in England, as noted earlier, were not established as a result of an overt public demand. Public demand, where it existed at all, was never more than latent, according to Kelly. (11) Both the proposers and the opponents of public libraries saw them as being essentially for the working classes. Only a few enlightened spirits—of whom Edward Edwards was one—recognised that libraries are for all classes. In actuality though, the majority of users in the early days of public libraries were in fact of the working and lower middle classes.

A marked sign that early British libraries were strongly educational in purpose was the amount of 'extension activities' they offered. In part, Kelly says, this was a carry-over from the mechanics' institutes and the literary societies, whose tradition the public libraries to some extent inherited. But essentially it arose from the conviction that public libraries were part of the educational system, and were therefore bound to do whatever lay in their power to promote educational work. Though most early public libraries were short of space, they still nevertheless attempted to provide public lectures, to organise science and art classes, and to encourage the activities of local cultural societies.

Their link with further education was strong. In Wolverhampton, for example, the Librarian, John Elliot, in 1873 arranged more than a score of evening classes, with nearly 350 students; and these classes continued under library control until 1902. Another example was the Watford Public Library and College of Science, Art, Music and Literature, which had Sir John Lubbock as its first President: here the welter of supplementary activities was such that it is said that the actual operation of the library itself suffered as a consequence.

There are some parallels between the British and American view of public libraries at this time. A striking quotation provided by Kelly from the *Middlesex courier* is a very echo of the American 'education, the gateway to equality and to success' philosophy described by C Seymour Thompson. The *Middlesex courier* declared: 'The library is the door-way of the knowledge which is power—power for success, for prosperity, and for honour'.

Kelly records that the years from Queen Victoria's Jubilee to the first world war were a time of tremendously rapid development in public library provision in Britain, the number of library authorities growing from 125 in 1886 to 549 in 1918, and the proportion of the population covered growing from about a quarter to about two-thirds. He adds: 'This dramatic expansion is in a way surprising, for although with the new emphasis on the educational needs of the nation public opinion was already by the beginning of the period better disposed than it had been towards public library development, attitudes were still by no means uniformly favourable'. But even so he is able to quote the splendidly supportive arguments of the committee at Willesden which in 1891 was organising the campaign for a public library: and in the context of the view that libraries have an educational purpose, that committee stated firmly that libraries 'provide the means of self-instruction for those who wish to learn . . . and the opportunity of research to the studious'.

Plainly though, views and attitudes relating to the educational purposes of libraries have constantly shifted and adjusted over the period since 1850. In our own times, for example, it is a fact that with such a plethora available of educational courses and institutions (full-time, part-time, sandwich courses, evening classes, by correspondence, or Open University) it would be difficult to build a case for the continuance of public libraries only on the basis of the residual need for unguided self-instruction. As far back as Edwards, it was not accepted that libraries should be 'direct educational agents themselves'; and in the 1920s, the Mitchell Report (1924); while acknowledging that libraries are educational, considered that 'the Public Library should not become in any sense a substitute for the ordinary recognised educational institution'.

There was a further shift of opinion in the 1950s and 1960s, when there emerged a strong distinction in library use between 'recreational' and 'purposive' use, reinforcing the physical separation of the 'general lending library' from the 'study and information' reference department. One reason for this, Kelly points out, was the rapid expansion in that period of secondary and higher education. By 1950 Lionel McColvin was expressing the belief that in future libraries would become more 'active' and 'purposive', and less concerned with 'that kind of recreational demand for which other agencies provide adequate substitutes'. His view was borne out by subsequent events—the spread of higher education; the growing complexity of society, government and technology; the new needs of industry and commerce; and the expansion of adult education.

Conversely though, there also came the growth of leisure and literacy, which increased the demand for recreational literature such as fiction, popular works on travel and biography, and books on sports and handicrafts. Radio and television, while certainly supplying a recreational demand, also had the apparently unexpected effect of stimulating book issues from public libraries rather than the reverse. And further to confound the earlier situation of public libraries being used for self-instruction by the lower classes, surveys after the second world war showed that public libraries had become increasingly middle-class in character.

4 THE DISSEMINATION OF KNOWLEDGE

It may be inferred from the foregoing section on society's views as to the real or supposed moral, social, political, educational and other effects of libraries, that libraries have now long been accepted as institutions for the dissemination of knowledge. If libraries had been regarded only as storehouses, none of these effects would have been postulated, because the knowledge which leads to them would have been inert. The principle stands that libraries are for both the storage and the dissemination of knowledge. It has of course been articulated by many librarians and historians of libraries.

At the beginning of this century, in 1910, Arthur E Bostwick, (12) contrasting the American 'modern library idea' with previous eras of library history, declared that the oldest libraries in the world were storehouses and 'did not conceive of their duties as extending to the entire community'. Bostwick is here surely employing a degree of poetic licence (or at least its equivalent in library history terms), because though indeed the library at Nineveh and the Alexandrian Library did not serve the entire community, they certainly were not administered solely as storehouses; his stricture is probably more justified in respect of the majority of the libraries of the Middle Ages. However, his essential and valid point is that American libraries have been conceived on the basis of the principle that their major purpose is the dissemination of knowledge.

Writing in 1930, Sir Frederic Kenyon, (13) having noted the 'acceptance of Public Libraries as part of the educational equipment of the country', goes on to describe them unequivocally—and he is here addressing a general, not a professional, audience in his brief, popular work—as 'the natural place of resort for information, for instruction, and for recreational reading'.

Raymond Irwin, writing in 1964, defines (14) what he considers the librarian's two main duties in terms of the principle that libraries are for the storage and dissemination of knowledge: 'First, he is the keeper or curator, charged with the task of preserving for future readers the books in his care. Secondly, he is the centre of the organic community which is the library, caring not merely for his books, but for the needs of every member of that community, and for the chain of recorded tradition which day by day is being handled, corrected, re-moulded, strengthened, added to, and passed onwards.'

Writing at the beginning of the present decade, in 1970, Elmer D Johnson (15) begins by defining a library as 'an organized collection of general information and literature', in which definition of course 'collection' equates with storehouse, and 'organised' (for use, that is) equates with dissemination. Johnson's definition of the 'fullest purpose' of libraries is 'making the heritage of the past fully available to all the people all the time'. He argues that modern European culture is a product of 'its preserved heritage in graphic form—in other words, of its libraries'. And he declares: 'The role of the library as an adjunct to education, as a device for information, as a partner to recreation, as a boon for business, or as an assistant to science, has been widely acclaimed and to a large extent realized'.

That libraries should disseminate knowledge as well as store it was of course argued for long before the beginning of the twentieth century, and the more important of these arguments have been rehearsed earlier in the present work, especially in the previous chapter on the question of access to libraries. The names of some of the most notable advocates will be recalled: Ashurbanipal, Gaius Asinius Pollio, Gabriel Naudé, John Durie, Thomas Bray, Panizzi, Edward Edwards. And of these John Durie coined the most memorable phrase, that a library which stored but which did not disseminate knowledge was 'a Talent digged in the ground', and as such, was useless.

References

1 Quoted in JOHNSON, E D: *History of libraries in the Western world*, 2nd ed, 1970.

2 CLARK, J W: *The care of books*, 1901.

3 COWTAN, R: *Memories of the British Museum*, 1872.

4 CARLYLE, T: *The hero as a man of letters*, 1840.

5 JOHNSON, E D: *op cit*, 1.

6 KELLY, T: *A history of public libraries in Great Britain, 1845-1965*, 1973.

7 EDWARDS, E: *Memoirs of libraries*, 1859.

8 THOMPSON, C S: *Evolution of the American public library, 1653-1876*, 1952.

9 EDWARDS, E: *op cit*, 7.

10 Quoted in MILLER, E: *Prince of librarians*, 1967.

11 KELLY, T: *op cit*, 6.

12 BOSTWICK, A E: *The American public library*, 1910.

13 KENYON, *Sir* F: *Libraries and museums*, 1930.

14 IRWIN, R: *The heritage of the English library*, 1964.

15 JOHNSON, E D: *op cit*, 1.

CHAPTER SIX

The role of the librarian

1 EARLY LIBRARIANS

In the mid-nineteenth century, a German Egyptologist, Karl Richard Lepsius, discovered at Thebes the tomb of two librarians who had served under Rameses. The librarians were named Miamum, father and son: the office being, like so many others in ancient Egypt, hereditary. And at the Temple of Thoth at Hermopolis, Johnson (1) tells us, where there was one of the largest collections of papyri on medical subjects, there was a scribe-priest whose title was 'Keeper of the Sacred Books', and who had as an assistant a woman librarian with the title 'Lady of Letters, Mistress of the House of Books'. Johnson adds that the librarians of ancient Egypt were important and highly educated persons, often of high political position.

It is chastening to realise, even from these scraps of information, how far back some of the essential elements in the foundation of the profession of librarianship stretch. A major principle, established therefore as early as the fourteenth century BC, is that a librarian must be a person of education. Another important principle is indicated in Johnson's reference to political position, but a more precise formulation of this must wait until the history of the role of the librarian is further surveyed in the present chapter. Even the fact that librarianship was hereditary in ancient Egypt tells us something about the real-life fortuituousness of recruitment into librarianship. There are even hints, which again will be developed later, of other aspects of the role of the librarian, in the phrases 'scribe-priest' and 'Keeper of the Sacred Books'. There is, in addition, confirmation that the role of the librarian should be considered an important one. And last, but by no means least, there is the factual evidence that librarianship did not start as an all-male profession: though it is curious to note that the familiar combination of a male chief and a female deputy is a three thousand year-old feature of the profession.

Going back to the clay-tablet libraries of Babylonia and Assyria which existed a thousand years even before the library at Nineveh, James Westfall Thompson tells us (2) that their librarians bore the title *Nisu-duppi-satri*, 'Man of the written tablets', and that the earliest known of these was a Babylonian called Amil-anu, who lived during the reign of Emuq-sin. Johnson fills in some detail here, by explaining that such librarians were of necessity well-trained. They had to be graduates of the school for scribes, and thoroughly trained in the literature or type of records they were to keep. After that, they served an apprenticeship for a number of years, learning 'the trade of librarian' (Johnson's phrase) and several languages at the same time. In addition to serving as librarians, these trained and polylingual individuals were often called on to edit, transcribe, and translate works needed by higher government or religious officials. In the temple libraries the librarian was a priest, often of high rank, while in the palace libraries he was an important official. In either case, adds Johnson, he was usually of the upper classes, and frequently the younger son of a noble family.

Again the brief information available about the early librarians of Babylonia and Assyria points to a set of consistent principles. The principle that a librarian must be a person of education is endorsed by the requirement in Babylonia that he should be a polylinguist and a specialist in some branch of literature or type of record. A further principle which emerges is that a librarian needs training and/or apprenticeship:

not only had these early Babylonian librarians to attend the school for scribes, but they had then to be apprenticed in a library for some years. There also occurs again the librarian/ priest connection, but since this was an alternative to the librarian/important government official combination, it must be deduced that the true connection is that of the librarian with power, whether religious or secular. Libraries are centres of power because knowledge is, and always has been, power. A less vital piece of evidence is the fact that in ancient Babylonia and Assyria, librarians were drawn from the upper classes, and frequently were younger sons: this of course endorses the connection of libraries with power, but it also demonstrates that recruitment to the profession through the ages has never been consistently from only one class or group.

More significant is the question of the importance of the role of the librarian. The fact that libraries are centres of power does not of itself make the librarian's role an important one. It will be seen that both the librarians of ancient Egypt and the librarians of ancient Babylonia and Assyria combined with their librarianship high-ranking importance in priestly or government roles. Their role as librarian was either an adjunct to other powerful roles, or their role as librarian was the power base for other important roles. It would seem therefore that any principle which might be formulated regarding the importance of the role of the librarian, on the historical evidence so far surveyed, would have to accommodate the concept that a librarian's role can only be an important one if it is fully integrated into the prevailing social and political system. This also means of course that librarians and libraries can never afford to be inward-looking only—as they were, for example, in Europe during the Middle Ages. It often appears therefore in this survey of the history of the principles of librarianship, that it was during the Middle Ages —not before—that librarianship picked up most of its bad habits. The chained book is symbolic in almost too many ways.

After the libraries of ancient Egypt, Babylonia and Assyria, came of course the Alexandrian Library, the first librarian of which appears to have been Demetrios of Phaleron, born c354-348BC. Demetrios was a philosopher who, while still young, was appointed governor of Athens, the affairs of which he administered for the ten years 317-307BC. Nothing is known of the next ten years of his life, but in 197BC Ptolemy Soter managed to induce him to come and live in Alexandria. When Ptolemy Soter died in 283BC, Demetrios was banished by Ptolemy II to Busiris in Upper Egypt.

It was Demetrios who suggested to Ptolemy Soter the establishment of a Museum, 'a meeting-place where the scholars of the earth should foregather to fix the canons of letters and to extend the scientific horizons of man'. (3) He also suggested to Ptolemy the founding of the Alexandrian Library. He was the King's Librarian, or the Director of the Library, or Keeper of the Books. In less than twelve years he collected 200,000 rolls and laid the vast foundation of the Library.

Demetrios was a man of style, power and presence; a scholar and versatile writer; and in the words of E A Parsons, a 'handsome, cultured Athenian man of letters and man of the world'. His successor as librarian was Zenodotus of Ephesus, who promoted 'free public access' (4) to the Library. The successor of Zenodotus as librarian was probably Callimachus of Cyrene, 'a universal scholar, the Father of Bibliography, the greatest bookman of his age'. (5)

James Westfall Thompson, (6) having commented that 'the most famous savants were in charge of the library of Alexandria', tells us that the heads of its major divisions were called *procuratores*, lesser employees *bibliothecarii*, assistants were designated as *a bibliotheca*, copyists as *antiquarii*, and archivists were known as *bibliophulakes*. The ordinary attendants were slaves owned by the state (*publici*), and were so numerous that they had their own doctor. He adds that the procurators 'were never directly called librarians for the reason that they were government officials who also had other duties, especially financial. But they were not mere finance officials, for the same men were also imperial secretaries for the Greek correspondence, or councillors of the emperor's studies (*a studiis*), and hence learned men. They belonged to the class of knights and received a salary of 60,000 sesterces. Real grammarians are mentioned as library administrators; as, for instance, Dionysius of Alexandria.'

The foregoing account of the Alexandrian Library unequivocally endorses the principle that librarians must be persons of education, and the attributes and status of Demetrios himself certainly add to the formulation of a principle relating to the importance of the role of the librarian. Demetrios was a highly-placed adviser in the court of Ptolemy Soter, and his position as such enhanced his role as librarian. The achievements of the Alexandrian Library required political support as well as professional skill. A further characteristic of Demetrios—which, as will be seen later, was shared by such great names as Panizzi and Melvil Dewey—was his supreme administrative ability. Another point which emerges is the need for a hierarchy of library staff. It is an error of modern times that in libraries it appears to be assumed that every single member of staff has to be educated and trained to the same high level—a policy as absurd as if all employees in a hospital were expected to be qualified as doctors.

In ancient Rome, librarians were not, in Johnson's opinion, (7) equal in importance to those of Alexandria. The numerous public libraries were administered in the name of the emperor by a *procurator bibliothecarum*, a post generally conferred upon some recognised scholar. In the time of Hadrian, for example, as James Westfall Thompson tells us, the directorship of the Greek and Latin libraries in Rome was held by the sophist L Julius Vestimus. Under the *procurator bibliothecarum*, each individual library had its own librarian (*bibliothecarius*), who was essentially an administrative officer. The position of *bibliothecarius* therefore became a political appointment or a civil-service post, with the real work of the library being performed by well-educated but less important assistants. These assistants bore a variety of titles: *librarius, vilicus,* or *antiquarius*. The *librarius*, says

106

Johnson, 'seems to have been a worker of various duties, from cataloguer to copyist, and from translator to clerical worker'. The *vilicus* was a general attendant, between custodial and clerical; the *antiquarius*, the scholar-librarian, historian and paleographer. The libraries were apparently administratively tightly-structured, with a variety of specialists and grades of staff in particular types of activity.

The arrangements so described seem to represent a fall from grace in the role of the librarian. First of all, the director of the whole system has become primarily a scholar; the individual library chief is no more than a civil servant; and the professional side of librarianship has become low-ranking. The only worthwhile heritage from the previous great libraries was the retention of the principle that a librarian must be a person of education.

The Middle Ages saw a continuation of this fall from grace in the role of the librarian. In the early universities, librarians did not even emerge as a professional class. Central libraries as such did not exist in most universities. Libraries were developed by the individual schools and colleges: at the University of Paris, more than fifty of these, each with its own library, were established over the years. Not until the nineteenth century did that university create a central library, with the Sorbonne Library as its nucleus.

The keeper of the books in these individual libraries was either a minor member of the academic staff, or a monk, or even a student. At Oxford, the books were left to the care of the chaplain. John Willis Clark recounts (8) that in 1367, the University passed a statute relating to the benefaction of Thomas Cobham, 'directing that Bishop Cobham's books are to be chained, in proper order; and that the Scholars who wish to use them are to have free access to them at convenient hours (*temporibus opportunis*). Lastly, certain volumes, of greater value, are to be sold, to the value of forty pounds, or more, if a larger sum can be obtained for them, for the purpose of purchasing an annual rent-charge of sixty shillings, to be paid to a chaplain, who is to pray for the soul of the aforesaid Thomas Cobham, and other benefactors; and who is to take charge of the books given by him and them, and of all other books heretofore given, or hereafter to be given, to the University. The passing of this statute may probably be regarded as the first institution of the office of University Librarian.'

What did develop in the Middle Ages was a strong emphasis on the technical skills of librarianship, and it is this emphasis which has been professionally the hardest to shuck off in subsequent eras. `John L Thornton did not perhaps realise that he was describing a situation of mixed blessing when he wrote of mediaeval libraries in the following terms: (9) 'In Europe the most prominent founders of libraries were the monks. Whenever a monastery was built, it quickly developed a library, and to the monks we are deeply indebted for the preservation of many valuable writings. They duplicated the manuscripts by laboriously copying them by hand, and much of our library technique is based on their methods.'

Then again, we have in the Customs of St Augustine, written between 1310 and 1344, what amounts to a description of mediaeval service to readers. In the Customs it is set down that the care of the book-presses is to be entrusted to the Precentor and his subordinate the Succentor. The former is to have his seat in front of the press and his own carrel near at hand. The Succentor is to have his seat and his carrel on the bench near the press (a bench commonly ran along the cloister wall). These arrangements were to make sure that the two officers, or at least one of them, were always at hand to be of service to the brethren.

The picture so described has a considerable degree of charm, but is most certainly not an image of power.

2 THE GROWTH OF THE PROFESSION

It is generally accepted that the first modern treatise on library science was Gabriel Naudé's *Avis pour dresser une bibliothèque*, published in 1627, and translated by John Evelyn in 1661 as *Instructions concerning erecting of a library*. Naudé's importance as a pioneer has already been referred to many times in preceding chapters; but the seventeenth century also saw in 1650 the publication of John Durie's *The reformed librarie-keeper*, and it was Durie who had most to say on the essential role of the librarian.

The first principle he enunciated was that a librarian is an educator. He complained that in his own time, 'The Librarie-Keeper's place and Office . . . are lookt upon, as Places of profit and gain . . . their places are but Mercenarie, and their employment of little or no use further, then to look to the Books committed to their custodie, that they may not bee lost; or embezzled by those that use them; and this is all'. Never, surely, has there been a more cutting indictment of the librarian who is not personally committed to his profession (but only occupying his place for a livelihood), and who sees his duties as not going beyond the mere custody of his books. Durie is harshly critical of those who pursue a career in librarianship merely on the basis that it purchases 'an easie subsistence; and some credit in comparison of others'. He concludes this line of argument by stating his first principle: 'For if Librarie-Keepers did understand themselves in the nature of their work, and would make themselves as they ought to bee, useful in their places in a publick waie; they ought to becom Agents for the advancement of universal Learning . . . '

It is worth recalling that Durie's belief in this principle that a librarian is an educator was echoed by Henry Evelyn Bliss (10) more than three hundred years later, when he dedicated his work on the organisation of knowledge in libraries to the librarian 'who is organizer and educator'. It was also the main principle which motivated the careers of Edward Edwards and Melvil Dewey, in particular, as will be seen in two subsequent sections of the present chapter.

Durie summed up his view of the role of librarian as follows: 'The proper charge then of the Honorarie Librarie-Keeper in an Universitie should bee thought upon, and the end of that Imploiment, in my conception, is to keep the publick stock of Learning, which is in Books and Manuscripts to increase it, and to propose it to others in the waie which may bee most useful unto all; his work then is to bee a Factor and Trader for helps to Learning, and a Treasurer to keep them, and a dispenser to applie them to use, or to see them well used, or at least not abused'.

He stresses this need for a librarian to increase his stock of books and manuscripts even to the extent of suggesting that his performance in this respect should be judged once a year by 'the chief Doctors of each facultie of the Universitie'. The Doctors should receive 'the Accounts of his Trading, that hee may shew them wherein the stock of Learning hath been increased, for that year's space'. The reader may recall the quotation in chapter two of the present work of a monastic rule to the effect that: 'The first duty of a librarian is to strive, in his time, as far as possible, to increase the library committed to him'. It was also made plain in that same chapter that such a rule has been followed by every great librarian. Another historic principle of librarianship can therefore be firmly stated: it is a librarian's duty to increase the stock of his library.

The most rapid development of the role of the librarian in modern times began in the nineteenth century, but before any survey of this development, some mention must be made of the views on the role of the librarian of that great precursor, Edward Edwards. In his *Memoirs of libraries* (1859), Edwards points out that a 'librarian' can preside over the Bodleian Library, or rule a Village Reading-Room. The former, he says, would need to be a scholar; the latter, no more than a ready and obedient drudge, a eunuch sitting at the door of an Eastern Harem. The 'root-qualities', though, he maintains, are the same in both instances: each of these two librarians must be '(1) a lover of books; (2) a man of methodical habits and of an organizing mind; (3) a man of genial temper and of courteous demeanour'.

Edwards continues this modest approach by complaining that 'to the common eye' the duties of librarianship look 'much easier than they are'. He comments that librarianship requires a personal discipline of a very harsh kind, since it appears to be a thankless task, difficult to perform well and rarely appreciated by those outside the profession. But though he retains his modest tone, Edwards is nevertheless quite definite about the principle that a librarian is an educator, and he describes thus what the profession of librarianship would offer an individual: 'It will never open for him a path to wealth or popular fame. It is, and is likely to be, eminently exposed to social indifference and misconception. But, as a means of permanent usefulness, it presents opportunities which are surpassed only by those of the Pulpit or the Press. By the enlightened and zealous discharge of its functions, a man's work may be made to carry within it the unfailing seeds of many mental harvests, only to be fully gathered in, when he shall have long lain in his grave.'

Still in modest vein, Edwards observes that librarianship should not be regarded as a respectable sort of 'refuge for the destitute', nor as the 'reward of suffering merit'; but he does show his teeth when he adds that 'it is not out of every sort of wood, that you can make a Librarian'. In conclusion he reminds librarians that even if their pleasure in books occasionally clouds over, they should always remember that they are performing an honest, worthwhile task, and that they can have a 'divinely appointed place in that mighty labour of Human Culture and Human Discipline which began at the outer gate of Eden, and will have no ending until Time shall be no more'.

It may be somewhat disappointing to find Edwards, that fiery educator and proponent of free public libraries, so muted in his analysis of the role of the librarian. It is however the case that Edwards expended most of his fire and most of his energies on educational and public library campaigns, very much at the expense of his own career as a librarian. It was subsequent to Edwards in the nineteenth century that the modern development of the role of the librarian began.

In the beginning, most public librarians in Britain in the mid-nineteenth century period had had no previous experience of librarianship. Though Edwards himself at Manchester had been trained in the British Museum, and J D Mullins at Birmingham had come from the Birmingham Subscription Library, most other places were either less fortunate or less enlightened. Liverpool appointed as its first Librarian a schoolmaster, J S Dalton; Oxford appointed a bookseller, B H Blackwell; Cambridge a twenty-two year old bookseller's assistant, John Pink (the runner-up for the appointment being a retired stage-coachman, who was defeated only by the casting-vote of the chairman); and Sheffield, a twenty-year old silverplater's apprentice, Walter Parsonson. Kelly notes (11) that many of these 'amateur public librarians' did very well; but it should be remembered that in its early years, public librarianship was indeed a humble task: long hours (often twelve hours a day or more), poor salary and lowly status. Nowhere was the librarian regarded as a professional man, but merely as the servant of the local library committee. All the planning of and initiative for library services came from the committee, with the librarian carrying out its instructions to the letter.

By the 1870s in Britain though, a great change was evident. The first generation of librarians had learned their job, and had trained up a body of assistants from which future librarians could be chosen: for example, James Yates, who in 1870 became the first Librarian of Leeds, came from the Bolton Library.

The 1870s also saw the founding, first, of the American Library Association in 1876, and then, in 1877, in Britain, of the Library Association. However, possibly the first convention of librarians in the world was that held in New York on September 15 1853. The call to this convention read: 'The undersigned, believing that the knowledge of Books, and the foundation and management of collections of them for public use, may be promoted by consultation and concert among librarians and others interested in bibliography, respectfully invite such persons to meet in Convention'. Eighty-two people attended the meeting, and concerned themselves with some very practical matters: among other things, the new edition of Poole's *Index to periodical literature*, the system of cataloguing employed at the Smithsonian Institution, and the need for a manual of information and suggestions on the organisation and management of small libraries.

No further convention was held in America until twenty-three years later, when on October 4 1876 a meeting of librarians in Philadelphia led to the founding of the American Library Association. By 1876 librarians realised that (in the words used at the time) 'the difficult and delicate art of library management rested upon a science'. The constantly increasing collections of the large libraries had made the problems of classification, cataloguing and administration more pressing and more difficult. A concerted effort, and a sharing of ideas and experience, were now greatly needed. And so at the 1876 meeting, Melvil Dewey moved that an Association be formed, and this motion was carried after being amended to provide that the constitution should include the following preamble: 'for the purpose of promoting the library interests of the country, and of increasing reciprocity of intelligence and good-will among librarians and all interested in library economy and bibliographical studies, the undersigned form themselves into a body to be known as the American Library Association'.

The first President of the new association, Justin Winsor, pleaded for the necessity of developing a science of library administration, a 'bibliothecal science'. 'We came together,' he said some years later, 'largely pervaded with the idea that a library was in essentials a missionary influence; that the power which belonged to it needed consolidating and directing, and that the first step in such work was for librarians to become acquainted with one another. To that end, and almost without any definite plan of cooperation, we first met; sealed our friendships; proclaimed our existence; measured our strength, and planned to set about our work.' (12)

113

Six years later in England, at the 1882 conference of the Library Association, H R Tedder addressed himself to the subject of librarianship as a profession. He was not content with Edwards's modest prescription of 'a lover of Books' with 'methodical habits and . . . organizing mind', but stressed the need—just as it had been stressed in the library world of ancient Babylonia—for training and/or apprenticeship. 'Without going into particulars,' he declared, 'one may expect the ordinary librarian to be a man of refinement, of liberal education, and especially endowed with sympathy with books and reading. But a general taste for literature is not all that is required . . . . To be thoroughly qualified a librarian should have had the practical experience of library work which it is impossible to obtain from any amount of book-reading, and if without experience he must possess the faculty of teaching himself. He should be a man of business habits and a good administrator; above all, he must be willing to devote his whole life to the study of his profession, for a librarian should never consider that he has finished his education. These requirements imply qualifications of a somewhat higher character than may perhaps be needed in all libraries, but some knowledge of languages and literatures, of bibliography, bibliology, and general library management, must be possessed by any person holding the chief position in the administration of a library, however small this may be.' (13)

Even after the turn of the century, James Duff Brown in his *Manual of library economy* (1903) was still having to warn library committees against 'the blunder of appointing chief librarians from the ranks of stickit ministers, unlucky schoolmasters, returned soldiers, minor journalists, unsuccessful booksellers, dilettante town councillors or such-like remnants of the failures or superannuated in other walks of life'. (14) Brown argued that the attributes required for the role of librarian included a wide knowledge of literature, bibliography and languages, plus an understanding of classification, cataloguing and library routine. And a few years later, in 1910, Arthur E Bostwick was writing in similar

114

vein: (15) 'Whether librarianship has yet arrived at the dignity of a profession is a moot point. There is no doubt, however, that it belongs to that class of occupations that require general culture, special training in theory, and practical experience.'

3 THE BEGINNINGS OF PROFESSIONAL EDUCATION

As early as 1859, in his *Memoirs of libraries*, Edward Edwards had thought that a 'Librarians' Association' would be a good idea, and he had confidently expected that one would eventually be formed in England. He stressed, though, that in his opinion it would never amount to anything unless it brought with it 'increased means of systematic study, and of public evidence of the fruits of study'.

In due course, as has been seen, a Library Association was founded, and at its conference in 1882 proposals were agreed for the formal training of librarians. The proposals involved three certificates based on examination:

1 A Preliminary Certificate, to be taken before entry to library work, requiring competence in arithmetic, English grammar and composition, English history, geography, English literature, and at least one foreign language.

2 A Second Class Certificate, to be given after not less than one year's library work, and requiring a knowledge of English literature, one other European literature, the principles of classification, the elements of bibliography and cataloguing, library management, and a cataloguing knowledge of at least two foreign languages.

3 A First Class Certificate, available to assistants of at least two years' standing, requiring a more advanced knowledge of the subjects studied for the Second Class Certificate, with a paper on general literary history. At this stage a cataloguing knowledge of at least three foreign languages was required. (16)

The first examinations for these certificates were organised by the Library Association at London and Nottingham in 1885. Revised schemes were introduced in 1891 and 1894, but it was not until a new syllabus was brought into operation in 1904 that candidates really began to come forward in even minor numbers. The 1904 syllabus covered six subjects: literary history, bibliography, classification, cataloguing, library history and organisation, and library administration. For each subject there was a separate examination, and an essay. Candidates were awarded a certificate for each subject successfully completed; and those who obtained certificates in all six subjects, and who had three years' approved library experience, were entitled to receive the Diploma of the Library Association. In 1907 the Library Association decided that Diploma candidates should also have to submit a thesis showing original thought or research, plus a certificate of competence in Latin or a modern foreign language. ·

However, ten years after the introduction of the 1907 scheme only twelve diplomas had been awarded while the certificate examinations, which had attracted 39 candidates in 1904, still were attracting only 313, ten years later, in 1914. Kelly points out that the main problem here was lack of teaching, candidates having by and large to work on their own. The Library Association made some effort to meet this need, and from 1893 a number of summer schools, classes and correspondence courses were instituted, first in London, and then in the larger provincial cities. In 1895 the Library Assistants' Association was founded, and this association helped those studying for librarianship examinations by arranging meetings and study circles, forming a library, and publishing a journal, the *Library assistant*.

In London from 1902, courses in librarianship were offered in collaboration with the London School of Economics. Finally, in 1919, with the aid of a five-year grant from the Carnegie Trust, the first full-time School of Librarianship was established at University College, London.

The Library Association, which received its charter in 1898, in 1909 set up an official register of librarians, ranging from Fellows (chief librarians and other senior officers, and holders of the Diploma), through Members (experienced and qualified

116

librarians not eligible for the Fellowship) and Associate Members (other members of library staffs and non-librarians), to student members (those under the age of twenty-five).

In the United States, the first formal course in librarianship was organised in the Library of Columbia University, New York, by its Librarian, Melvil Dewey, in 1887. Bostwick, writing in 1910, (17) notes that there were by that time three kinds of courses available: library schools (affiliated to a university, or some other educational institution, or to a library); summer schools (short courses); and training classes (local and special, a sort of systematisation of apprenticeship). He also refers to the two-year course at the New York State school, for college graduates only, leading to the degree of BLS (Bachelor of Library Science), the work for each of the two years being divided into four parts: administrative, bibliographic, practical and technical.

4 WOMEN IN LIBRARIANSHIP

Just as the hiatus in library history between the library school in Babylonia and the re-emergence of library schools in the late nineteenth/early twentieth century in Britain and America is a long one, so also is the hiatus in the re-appearance of women in librarianship from ancient times (notably the Egyptian 'Mistress of the House of Books' at the Temple of Thoth at Hermopolis) until the latter half of the nineteenth century in England and America.

Kelly recounts (18) that the employment of women assistants in public libraries in England seems to have begun in 1871 at Manchester, as an expedient to overcome the shortage of suitable young men. The experiment was a success: the women assistants were good at their job, and cheaper than men. By 1879, Manchester was employing 31 women assistants. This trend was however slow to develop elsewhere—in the public library at Leeds, for example, women assistants were not employed until 1898.

Nevertheless, the one hundred years since 1871 have witnessed in Britain an increasing momentum in the recruitment of women into librarianship. During the five-year period from 1970, for example, Patricia Layzell Ward reports (19) that of students attending United Kingdom library schools, nearly three-quarters were women. Even more striking are the figures which she provides of individuals seeking election to the Register of chartered librarians during the period 1947 to 1972—in 1947, 45 per cent were men; but by 1972, this percentage had dropped to 28 per cent. However, she also adds that of the chief librarians of this country in the mid-1970s, not more than half-a-dozen were women.

In America, women came into librarianship relatively early in the development of the profession. The first women clerks were employed in the Boston Public Library when that institution was established in 1852, and the first woman librarian was appointed by the Boston Athenaeum in 1857. By 1870, 20 per cent of the librarians in the United States were women. By 1910, librarianship was fully established as a woman's profession: 75 per cent of all librarians then were women. By 1970, this percentage had risen even higher—to 82 per cent.

It is also worth recalling, as Anita Schiller notes, (20) that when Melvil Dewey established the first American library school at Columbia University in 1887, 17 out of the 20 entrants were women: though, incidentally, this admissions policy of Dewey resulted in his dismissal and the demise of the school (which Dewey moved to Albany subsequently).

Schiller's main argument is that currently women are being systematically eliminated from leadership positions in an occupation in which they constitute four-fifths of the membership. She quotes recent figures which demonstrate that despite this preponderance of women in librarianship in the United States—80 per cent in general, among school librarians 94 per cent, among public librarians 87 per cent, among special librarians 72 per cent, among academic librarians 67 per cent—the higher salaries and the top positions still go to men. She mentions that in the Library of Congress in 1972, of the librarians at the beginning position for

118

individuals with a master's degree in library science, 54 per cent were women; but at the top of the personnel pyramid, in the 'supergrade positions', the percentage held by women was only 4 per cent; and at the very highest level (3 posts), there were no women at all.

Schiller reports that the national pattern in America is that the librarians of large cities and large academic institutions are invariably men, while librarians of smaller cities and smaller colleges tend to be women. The curious thing, as she notes, is that this is a recent trend. There were more women in top library positions in the 1920s than there are in the 1970s. In some ways the reason seems to be that libraries and library budgets have become so much more important that the appointment of a man has been felt to be necessary.

Schiller also reminds us of the school of thought which blames the 'weakness' and 'disadvantaged condition' of librarianship as a career on the preponderance of women in it: on its 'feminization'. What we have here is a 'Which came first, the chicken or the egg?' type of argument. Were women recruited into librarianship because it was a weak and disadvantaged one; or did the high proportion of women pursuing it as a career cause it to become, like their own position in society, weak and disadvantaged? Schiller is unable to resolve this particular poser; but she does point out that it was not the preponderance of women in librarianship which produced low salaries, but rather that the low salaries in librarianship attracted only women. Nevertheless she finds it harder to contest the allegation that the 'bureaucracy, hierarchy, and lack of autonomy' in the profession is to be blamed on the preponderance of women in it.

Schiller's final note is a more sanguine one. She is convinced that the current position of women in librarianship is being beneficially affected by 'the sweeping national impact of the women's movement'.

5 INDIVIDUAL LIBRARIANS

Sir Frederic Kenyon, in his brief history of libraries, (21), draws attention to 'the human element in the making and use of libraries'. He declares: 'Libraries have been formed by men and are administered by men for the use of men; and in the history of libraries it is individual men that have led the way'. Kenyon then recalls some of the great individual names: Callimachus, Thomas James, Humphrey Wanley, Gabriel Naudé, Nicholas Colbert, Antonio Panizzi, Edward Edwards, James Duff Brown. The last sections of the present chapter will be devoted to two of these—Edward Edwards and Antonio Panizzi—plus a third, the great American librarian, Melvil Dewey; but as a preliminary, some general comments on the contribution of individual librarians are called for.

Kenyon himself notes that 'the Public Libraries have owed nothing to public demand, but everything to individual initiative and enthusiasm'. Here he is undoubtedly referring to that very long line of committed and visionary public librarians of whom the first in Britain was Edward Edwards, and among the latter, in our own century, Lionel McColvin. In similar vein, Elmer D Johnson has observed (22) that libraries tend to be formed by individual efforts, either selfishly or for the benefit of the community, and not by people as a majority of the community.

What makes an individual a great librarian may in some degree be revealed by the brief examination later in this chapter of the lives of Edwards, Panizzi and Dewey. However, greatness does not appear to rest solely on technical competence. As Raymond Irwin commented: (23) 'If, indeed, there is one lesson that the history of libraries teaches us, it is that something over and above technical knowledge is needed to make the great librarian: a library cannot live on librarianship alone'.

Kenyon believed that 'librarians must be educated men. The ideal librarian would be a man of universal knowledge, unlimited sympathies, inexhaustible patience and tact, and an accomplished administrator.' In making such a statement Kenyon must, like Irwin, have had an eye to the history of libraries: for indeed all great individual librarians have been educated men; most have had 'unlimited sympathies'; all have necessarily been patient, but not all have been tactful; and, true enough, the majority have been gifted administrators.

W C Berwick Sayers has reflected (24) that each country in turn seems to produce a distinctive librarian who is the prototype of his profession. The examples which came to his mind were Edward Edwards and James Duff Brown in Great Britain, Melvil Dewey in America, Arnim Graesel in Germany, Léopold Victor de Lisle in France, Paul Otlet in Belgium, and Shiyali Ramarita Ranganathan in India. Sayer's theme could be further embroidered, for each country seems to produce librarians with quite distinctive, almost national, characteristics. Dewey was as we think most American librarians to be—practical and vigorous; Edwards and Brown were sturdy and well-meaning; Ranganathan was ingenious, convoluted, charismatic.

Ranganathan, as the accepted 'father of librarianship in India', merits at least a brief note. He was born in 1892, and after graduation lectured in mathematics in the Government College, Madras, for three years, subsequently becoming (1920-1923) assistant professor of mathematics in the Presidency College, Madras. Then, without previous library experience, he was appointed Librarian of Madras University, and sent to England to study methods at the British Museum. He attended the University of London School of Librarianship, where he studied library administration, and classification under W C Berwick Sayers himself. Ranganathan eventually returned to Madras fired with the intention of improving and extending library provision in India. He founded the Madras Library Association, and in 1928 delivered a university examination course to nearly one thousand teachers on library science, which led to the founding in the following year of the first Madras Summer School of Library Science. Subsequently, for twenty years, he combined his librarianship of the University with his headship of the school. Then after two years as University Librarian and Professor of Library Science at Benares Hindu University, he was from 1947 to 1955 Professor of Library Science in the University of Delhi.

Ranganathan was a charismatic lecturer, and travelled the world. He formulated an approach to library classification which has attracted numerous adherents. He wrote prolifically and freshly on all aspects of librarianship. Basically, though, he did what all great librarians do, as Edward Edwards did, and as Melvil Dewey did: he drew attention, on a remarkable scale, to the power and importance in society of libraries and librarianship. He was, in his time, like Edwards and Dewey in theirs, a one-man crusade.

In addition to Dewey, of course, America has produced a very considerable number of great librarians. Fremont Rider has pointed out (25) that most of our present-day library techniques were crystallised by American pioneers such as Dewey, Charles Ammi Cutter (1837-1903) and William Frederick Poole (1821-1894). To this list of great American librarians (and again starting with Dewey) Charles A Goodrum (26) adds George H Baker (1850-1911) of Columbia University, John Cotton Dana (1856-1929) from Newark, and William I Fletcher (1844-1917) of Amherst. 'These men,' writes Goodrum, 'were the very antithesis of the popular image of the timid bookman. They were zealots, dogmatic and doctrinaire, for whom all bibliothecal matters were either jet black or lily white.'

Goodrum is here contrasting this particular breed of librarian with the first great Librarian of Congress, Ainsworth Rand Spofford. Spofford, appointed in 1864, was (in Goodrum's phrase) 'the Cecil Rhodes of the institution'. He dedicated his thirty-three years as Librarian to making the Library of Congress the national library. He amassed a great collection and secured a building for it that was immense for its day. He was more interested in the acquisition of material than in its cataloguing or availability for reference use. As Goodrum says: 'Poor Mr Spofford symbolized all the things that distressed the new men most. They believed in rational order so that any scholar or any man in the street could enter their libraries and quickly find precisely what he sought and take it with him. Mr Spofford was so casual about order that when his 740,000 volumes were moved to the new building, barely one-third had been catalogued. They believed in uniformity. They were trying to work out a basic set of rules by which all books would be identified and all classified in a similar way. Mr Spofford felt no such obligation, and, as he shuffled his volumes into the forty-four classifications he had inherited, literally floors of volumes were mixed together in whatever organization he found most congenial at the time.'

The next great Librarian of Congress was Herbert Putnam (1861-1955), a man very much in the new mould: zealous, doctrinaire, organised. Goodrum supplies the following vivid pen-portrait: 'Putnam was a small, vital, red-haired man, with a bristling mustache, who is repeatedly referred to by his contemporaries as a patrician. His personality seems to have significance to our understanding of the Library because it appeared to have been the agent with which he steamrollered his way through staff, Congress, and his intellectual peers. He was rarely blocked or even resisted, and, on the few occasions when this occurred, his ability to outflank the opposition was impressive. We are asked to picture a man "aloof, remote, detached (with) impenetrable dignity". His associates describe him as "formal" (no one could ever recall his having been addressed by his first name, no subordinate was permitted to sit or take notes in his presence; orders were to be memorized as they were delivered).

'His relations with his staff were particularly intriguing. On the occasion of his retirement—having taken the Library from the Gay Nineties, through World War I, the Roaring Twenties, and the Depression, to the threshold of World War II—he was repeatedly lauded as "venerated". This in spite of the fact that for much of his career he paid his employees less than a dollar a day, that his salaries were dramatically lower than those for similar employees in Washington or in the library profession, and that he had resisted any form of civil service, job classification, or merit increases for years. Instead, we hear how he was able to infuse his staff "with a sense of mission, dedication, and their almost limitless opportunities for patriotic endeavor". Throughout his forty Library of Congress years, professionals begged to work for him for nothing in exchange for training and experience.

'He was a thoroughgoing bureaucrat but of a peculiarly perverse variety. On the one hand, while he hired, fired and paid each individual as he saw fit, on the other he was passionately fond of formal organization.'

Finally, mention must be made of the third great Librarian of Congress (from 1939 to 1944), Archibald MacLeish. Again, as with Putnam, the substance of the legend lies in the quality of his committed leadership. 'The employees he left behind,' comments Goodrum, 'compared the experience of having worked with him to having lived in the tail of a comet.'

6 EDWARD EDWARDS

Edward Edwards was born on December 14 1812, in Stepney, London, the son of a bricklayer-tiler, to whose trade he was apprenticed on his fourteenth birthday. There is no record of Edwards's schooling, or even evidence that he ever attended school. He appears to have owed his considerable education first to his mother, a woman of some education herself; then to the fact that he was a member of a Dissenting congregation; and also to the help of many friends, in particular Edwin Abbott (1808-1882), the Headmaster of Marylebone Philological School, who recognised Edwards as being a man of remarkable ability.

In October 1834 Edwards registered as a reader at the British Museum, which at that time was the only large library in London freely accessible to the public. It so happened that in March of the following year the House of Commons appointed a Select Committee 'to inquire into the condition, management and affairs of the British Museum', and when the minutes of the evidence were printed, Edwards published a seventy-six page pamphlet (addressed to the Radical MP Benjamin Hawes) entitled *Remarks on the Minutes of evidence*. The Select Committee, which had

124

adjourned in August 1835, was re-appointed in 1836, and Edwards himself was summoned to give evidence on June 2 1836. W A Munford, Edwards's most recent biographer, (27) notes that Edwards, in giving evidence to the committee, was very self-assured.

Edwards continued his interest in the British Museum after his evidence to the Select Committee, and wrote to Panizzi on library matters. Then in February 1839, Edwards was appointed as one of the temporary assistants for the preparation of the new catalogue.

All of this was no mean achievement for a self-made, self-taught bricklayer-tiler's son; but additionally, Edwards was not only continuing to increase his own education and scholarship (writing works, for example, on medals, and on New South Wales), but also promoting the education of others by involving himself in multifarious activities, such as work to do with the Central Society of Education, and the Art Union of London. It will be seen therefore that Edwards's career, from its very beginning, conformed with two of the main principles relating to the role of a librarian: namely, that a librarian must be a person of education; and that a librarian is an educator.

However, though Edwards (in the words of Greenwood)(28) 'had in him the essentials of a strong mind, and an individuality which impressed itself upon everything he undertook', he was also possessed of (in Munford's words) an 'extraordinary lack of self-discipline, which . . . made it as difficult for him to control the length of any of his published books or articles as to manage his private finances'. This serious defect in Edwards's temperament led him into difficulties not only with the Art Union (whose finances he was accused of mishandling), but with his new employer, Panizzi. Panizzi complained both about his unpunctuality and his cataloguing performance. Edwards was not an easy employee, and (in Panizzi's own words) argued a point 'with so much bitterness' as to make his colleagues 'risk losing their temper'. Panizzi wanted to dismiss Edwards in 1842, but was not successful in his attempt. Altogether, Edwards's time at the British Museum seems to have been a series of wrangles. In the end, it was obvious that either Edwards or Panizzi had to go; and in 1850, the Trustees dismissed Edwards.

In contrast with this background of bickering and petty discord was Edwards's conduct of his great campaign for free public libraries. The details of this campaign, culminating in the passing in 1850 of the Public Libraries Act, have already been recounted in chapter four. As Munford has written, it is to Edwards 'more than to any other man . . . we owe the municipal library in the form in which it has developed'. It is this achievement which marks out Edwards as a great librarian. It is the very embodiment of the established principle that a librarian's role can only be an important one if it is fully integrated into the prevailing social and political system. Edwards was entirely responsible, in tandem with William Ewart, MP, for the acceptance socially and politically in Britain of free public libraries.

After the apprenticeship in (and dismissal from) the British Museum Library, Edwards was appointed in 1851 Librarian of the Manchester Free Library at a (disappointing to him) salary of £200 per annum. Again though, it will be seen that Edwards's career conformed to another established principle: that a librarian must have training and/or apprenticeship.

He began in Manchester by compiling a draft list of some 5,000 books, described by Munford as 'a most useful and well-chosen collection'. Typically, he overspent his financial allocation for books, and this led to his first trouble with the Library Committee, in November 1851, when he made matters worse by being quite tactless in his discussions with its members. Trouble with his committee was a feature of Edwards's eight-year incumbency at Manchester. In the beginning, the committee met every week; and every committee member had the right to supervise Edwards's activities. This kind of surveillance by laymen must have been galling to the man who after all had planned the establishment of the municipal library system as such. Edwards was irascible by nature anyway: for example, while in Manchester, he once threw a copy of Pigot's *Directory* at a man who was trying to sell it to him, and was taken to court over the matter.

Edwards resented being the servant of his committee. His insubordinate and disrespectful attitude to certain of its members and his constant seeking for an improvement in his salary led eventually to a move by the committee in 1858 to seek his resignation, a move which (backed by Manchester Council) was in the end successful.

Edwards did try to defend himself on the strength of his considerable record of achievement at Manchester. He had built up a library, including a number of branches, which was very well used by the public; and he had managed to do this economically and without a large or qualified staff. He wished to be judged, he said, not by his 'shortcomings and mistakes', but by the 'broad results'. He had promoted an enlightened philosophy regarding municipal libraries, which he stated thus: 'They must be in no sense "Professional libraries" or "tradesmen's libraries" or "working men's libraries" but TOWN LIBRARIES. To that end they must contain, in fair proportions, the books that are attractive to the uneducated and the half-educated, as well as those which embrace the studies and assist the pursuits of the clergyman, the merchant, the politician and the professional scholar.'

But nevertheless, dismissed he was. Again, though, it may be noted that he conformed while in Manchester with yet another established principle of librarianship: by building up as he did a collection of some 50,000 volumes from scratch, he surely fulfilled his duty as a librarian to increase the stock of his library. And while in Manchester also, he confirmed his role as an educator in that, though in politics 'a radical of the Cobden school' (as a contemporary described him), he confined his political activities there to lending strong support to the Public School Association which was helping to prepare the way for the Education Act of 1870.

The aftermath of his Manchester period was difficult for Edwards. Munford characterises the period 1859 to 1870 as Edwards's 'Ishmaelite years': when he was obliged to scrape together a living in a variety of ways. He bought a partnership in a bookselling firm, but this lasted only a few months. He tried to live by his pen—for example, he produced an article on *Police* for the *Encyclopaedia Britannica*; a volume, *Liber de Hyda*, for the Rolls Series; and a two-volume life of Sir Walter Ralegh. More notably, he published in 1859 his two-volume *Memoirs of libraries*, basically the propagandist work of a librarian who saw (in Munford's words) the municipal free public library' as 'the highest and most socially significant form'. Apart from writing, Edwards also acted as a consultant on libraries and catalogues.

In general though, this period was one of poverty and ill-health for Edwards. Then in 1870, he was appointed to prepare a catalogue of the library of Queen's College, Oxford. In Oxford, Edwards found his spiritual home; and he enjoyed himself socially there also. After his work at Queen's College, he continued with temporary work at Corpus Christi College Library, and then at the Bodleian. On his appointment to the latter he was pictured in the following words: 'In his top hat and frock coat, and with his long white whiskers, he presented a very Victorian, if by now rather dilapidated figure'.

At the age of seventy, Edwards found himself unemployed again and in penury; but eventually he was granted a small Civil List pension. His last years were spent on the Isle of Wight, one of his favourite places; and there he continued to write and to study. At the very end of his life, however, such was his continuing incompetence in managing his financial affairs, that he was turned out of his lodgings—poor, in bad health, in debt, and relatively forgotten. He died in 1886.

Curiously, Edwards seemed to outlive his reputation. Though Melvil Dewey had written to Edwards in 1877 calling him 'the foremost writer and thinker in the library world', when E W B Nicholson took the initiative in that same year to organise in Britain a conference of librarians, he did not even know that Edwards was still alive—he knew him only as 'a

128

giant of the past'. Some amends were however made in 1882 when Edwards was elected an Honorary Member of the Library Association.

But a giant Edwards certainly was. Though his strong-mindedness, fixed views and powerful but undisciplined individuality caused him nothing but difficulties in his personal life, these same attributes in his public life revolutionised libraries and librarianship in Britain. And though he could hardly have been aware of it himself, the principles which guided him were the very same principles which had guided his greatest predecessors.

7 ANTONIO PANIZZI

It was a surprise to his contemporaries, and it has apparently remained a surprise ever since, that the greatest of British librarians should have been an Italian refugee. Indeed, on Panizzi's appointment in 1837 to the Keepership of the Printed Books in the British Museum there was much 'opposition and unkindly criticism . . . in the public press'. (29) But the fact is that Panizzi, as will be seen, epitomised every principle relating to the role of librarian: he was an educated man; he was an educator; he served a long apprenticeship in librarianship; he saw the role of librarian as being important socially and politically; and he fulfilled his duty as librarian to increase the stock of his library.

Antonio Genesio Maria Panizzi was born on September 16 1797, at Brescello in the Duchy of Modena, the son of a pharmacist. In 1814, at the age of seventeen, he entered the University of Parma. He had already been introduced to the world of books at the age of twelve, when he had attended the grammar school at Reggio, where Gaetano Fantuzzi, a former professor of rhetoric, was in charge of the communal library, and with whom Panizzi became friendly; in Parma, he likewise became friendly with Angelo Pezzana, the learned librarian of the Biblioteca Parmense, who influenced him and his life greatly.

Panizzi took his degree, in jurisprudence, in 1818, and was henceforth entitled to call himself 'Doctor', though he never used the prefix in his time in England. Perhaps his most noticeable characteristic at this period was, in the words of his most recent biographer, (30) his 'incredible application for study'.

He was appointed the equivalent of town clerk in his home town in 1819; but in 1822, he fled Italy for political reasons, arriving penniless in London in May 1823. He went subsequently to Liverpool, making his living there by teaching Italian. Eventually he was appointed to the Chair of Italian Language and Literature at the University of London in 1828; but this post was not sufficient to absorb his great energies and he was not happy in it.

Then in 1831, with the help of two influential friends, Henry Brougham and Thomas Grenville, he was appointed to the vacant Assistant Librarianship at the British Museum. Miller, his biographer, writes: 'At last Panizzi had entered an institution, where, for the first time, he could make truly felt his great talents and his prodigious powers of organisation'. (31) At that time the Department of Printed Books contained no more than some 240,000 books. Panizzi's first duties were in the field of cataloguing.

In 1835, the House of Commons resolved that a 'Select Committee be appointed to inquire into the condition, management and affairs of the British Museum'; but this committee was unable to report any resolutions to the House, and a new committee was appointed to continue the inquiry in the next session. It was to this committee that Panizzi gave evidence. His evidence was sensible and detailed, and included his two classic statements on the 'poor student' and on the educational purpose of the British Museum:

—'I want a poor student to have the same means of indulging his learned curiosity, of following his rational pursuits, of consulting the same authorities, of fathoming the most intricate inquiry as the richest man in the kingdom, as far as books go, and I contend that the Government is bound to give him the most liberal and unlimited assistance in this respect.'

—'As to its most important and most noble purpose as an establishment for the furtherance of education for study and research, the public seem to be, almost, indifferent.'

Panizzi's evidence dominated the committee. Miller pictures him as 'this brawny man of forty, with the face of a bandit'; Munford, in his book on Edward Edwards, (32) reports Edwards as being impressed by Panizzi's performance and as saying that Panizzi gave his evidence 'with an earnestness and with a vivacity and felicity of argument and of illustration'.

In 1837, as noted earlier, he was appointed Keeper of the Printed Books, but against some opposition: he was, after all, a papist, a revolutionary, and a foreigner. His first two jobs were to transfer the Library from old Montague House to the quarters that had been assigned to Printed Books in Sir Robert Smirke's new building at the north end of the Museum site; and to produce a new printed catalogue. But his ultimate objective was to make the Library supreme, not only in Great Britain, but throughout the world.

He annoyed the Trustees at the outset by overspending his grant, and by sticking to his own strong views on the proposed new catalogue. The Trustees interfered over even very small details, a situation which infuriated Panizzi. Panizzi's predicament is indeed reminiscent of that of Edwards in relation to the Library Committee at Manchester. Panizzi, however, succeeded eventually in overcoming the Trustee's contradictory and vascillating approach by 'a combination of skill, knowledge, resolution and experience'. (33)

Panizzi had two prime aims in view: to build up the Library by every means in his power, so as to make it the greatest and most representative collection on earth; and to make the books so acquired speedily and readily available to all readers. For the first, he needed proper enforcement of the Copyright Act, and active agents throughout Europe and the United States; for the second, more and better staff, the best catalogues available, and adequate accommodation. He eventually achieved the proper enforcement of the Copyright Act, and he did recruit agents; as for staffing and accommodation, the former steadily increased and improved, and the provision of the latter culminated in 1857 with the opening of the famous round Reading Room.

But meantime, in the 1840s, there was growing public discontent with and criticism of the British Museum, and of the Reading Room and the Department of Printed Books in particular: Panizzi's new regulations for readers were not liked, the printed catalogue had not appeared, and there were (in Miller's words again) 'dark suspicions of the library and of its foreign head'. To the outsider, the Museum 'seemed to be old-fashioned, incompetent and riddled with corruption'. The constant quarrels and ill-feelings amongst its members of staff were also well-known publicly—particularly the open warfare between Sir Frederic Madden, Keeper of the Department of Manuscripts, and Panizzi himself.

In 1847 a Royal Commission was appointed to inquire into the British Museum's affairs. Panizzi welcomed, even helped to promote, this investigation, because he felt the need to vindicate himself publicly. He also knew he was well represented by friends on the commission. The report of the commission, which appeared on March 28 1850, was a triumphant vindication of Panizzi, who also routed Edward Edwards (and his criticism of the British Museum Library) at the hearings in 1850 of the Select Committee on Public Libraries. Panizzi then stood supreme, in Miller's words 'the virtual master of the Museum'.

The culmination of Panizzi's power came in 1857. As mentioned earlier, the Library was in need of further accommodation even after its move to Sir Robert Smirke's new building; and on the evening of April 18 1852, Panizzi drew a rough pencil sketch which was the genesis of the great Reading Room. In March 1853 all purchase of books was suspended because there was no space for more: and in 1854 the Treasury finally approved the expenditure of £86,000 on Panizzi's scheme. The Reading Room took four years to build, Panizzi supervising every detail, no matter how small.

In May 1857 the Reading Room was formally opened, and this was indeed Panizzi's finest hour, because he was no longer merely Keeper of the Printed Books, but Principal Librarian of the British Museum.

Sir Frank Francis, in his introduction to Miller's biography, declares that 'the British Museum Library as most of us have known it is Panizzi's creation'; Panizzi was, he says, 'an administrator of genius'; and he notes 'the wide sweep of his activities . . . his bold generous spirit . . . his impatience of arrogance and incompetence . . . his pugnacious striving for the good of the British Museum . . . his unstinted loyalty'. Miller himself talks of Panizzi's 'superabundant energy', and of his 'resource, courage and integrity'. His blemishes, if such they are to be counted, were a quick temper; ambition; a consciousness of his own great abilities; the fact that he was (in Miller's words) 'a man whom, at any time it was dangerous to cross'; and that he could merit from William Ewart the epithet 'Stick-at-nothing-izzi'. All his attributes, good and bad, were well summed up by Constance Brooks (as quoted by Munford): 'He had a wonderful power of inspiring his subordinates with his own ardour and, though he sometimes let his naturally quick temper get the better of him, those who worked under him realized that, though he might swear at carelessness and severely reprimand laxity or lack of interest, he was the first to help those who showed a real interest and zest in their work'.

8 MELVIL DEWEY

Incontestably, Dewey is the best-known name in American librarianship. The chief reason, of course, is the universal use of the classification system devised by him and which bears his name; but Dewey's greatness as a librarian was wider-based than the mere invention of a classification scheme, and his commitment to librarianship was as total as that of Panizzi and Edwards. Fremont Rider, his biographer, (34) describes him as 'a genius', a 'dynamo of energy', a 'fifty-ton tank', a fighter: he was, declares Rider, 'the greatest man with whom I ever came into long-continued personal contact'.

Melville Louis Dewey was born on December 10 1851 at Adams Center, New York; his father was a man of some property and a variety of business interests. From the outset of his life, Dewey was a hard worker, always studying and reading, and with a passion for system and classification. He obtained a teaching certificate when he was still very young, and at the age of seventeen wrote in his diary: 'I have now fully decided to devote my life to education. I wish to inaugurate a higher education for the masses'.

Very early on, therefore he had adopted two of the main principles relating to the role of librarian: to educate himself, and to educate others. These were his dominating principles professionally: just as it can be said that the principle which dominated Panizzi's career was the increase of the stock of his library, and the principle which Edward Edwards most fully embraced was that relating to the integration of libraries into the prevailing social and political system.

Dewey graduated at Amherst College in 1874. He had begun working in the college library in his junior year, and while working there—and still an undergraduate and not yet twenty-two years old—he had drafted 'that great scheme for book classification with which his name will be forever linked' (Rider's words). After his graduation, he became acting librarian and served as such until 1876, the year in which the first edition of his classification was published.

He moved to Boston in 1876, and set up an office there. This period, from 1876 until 1883, was his most formative one. With Dewey as its secretary and chief moving spirit, the American Library Association, the first library organisation, was founded; the *Library journal*, the first library periodical, appeared under Dewey's editorship; the Dewey Decimal Classification began to spread abroad; and under Dewey's leadership and impetus, the Library Bureau—initiator of all sorts of new library devices and equipment—was established. As if all these were not enough, Dewey also embarked on the other two great interests of his life, metric reform and spelling reform. He was indeed, as Rider observes, a man of ideas and of 'indefatigable industry'. He even drew up 'time budgets' so as never to waste a moment.

In 1883, he was appointed Librarian of Columbia College, and he started there the modern world's first library school, almost on faith and enthusiasm alone, for Columbia was not too sure that it wanted it. The trustees of the College passed a resolution in 1884 setting up the Columbia College School of Library Economy, but gave Dewey no resources; they even tried to talk him out of it, but he battled fiercely. What aggravated the trustees even more subsequently was that Dewey's first class had more women in it than men—and Columbia was not co-educational. Dewey was not over-popular in any case because, for example, he believed that professors should pay fines on overdue books like everybody else; and because he was 'boastful and vigorous in his library reports' (Rider's words); and also because, generally, he was impatient and unwilling to follow accepted precedents.

But the school was duly opened, in 1887. It transformed the library profession in America; perhaps, as Rider argues, it even created it. Dewey's personality was the inspiration of the school; he believed that library work was not a job, but at once a sacred trust and a great opportunity for service. Dewey preached librarianship as a crusade: active, positive, vigorous—not lethargic or dawdling. As Herbert Putnam, Librarian of Congress, said of him some years later (in 1905): 'Mr Dewey eats, drinks, sleeps, and talks library and library work throughout the twenty-four hours, the week, the month, and the year'.

His stand on behalf of the cause of women in librarianship was valiant and remarkable. All his life, as Rider observes, he 'pleaded for an equal place for women, with men, in all the world's work'. One outcome of this stand along with others on various matters of principle, was that in 1889 his resignation as Columbia's Librarian was accepted by the trustees, he having been charged with 'gross insubordination'. Dewey moved his school to Albany in 1889, where it eventually became well-known as the New York State Library School.

Apart from running the school (which was closest to his heart), he was also State Librarian. As a footnote, it may be added that in 1926 Columbia University made amends to Dewey by taking the school back under its wing.

Dewey's life-long devotion to the cause of education also led him to spend eleven very busy years in educational administration, as Secretary of the New York State Board of Regents. He fought to bring about long overdue educational reforms, in the face of pressures and attacks of every kind. Rider talks of the 'aggressive fertility of his restless mind', and records that he did 'the work of a dozen men'. One of the Board of Regents' resolutions described him (despite the frictions and controversies which he continually caused) as 'an organiser of genius, an executive of great skill, an educational leader of marked originality and energy'. Also in the cause of education, Dewey founded the Lake Placid Club, a cooperative vacation-club which grew to be huge: Dewey himself described it as 'a university in the woods'.

Dewey's essential achievement though, as Rider stresses, was that he strove for sixty years, and strove successfully, to create not only a library profession but a library economy. As a librarian himself, Dewey was very effective at both Amherst and Columbia; he was indeed described by President Barnard of Columbia as 'the most accomplished librarian in the country' and as being 'in advance of public opinion'. He was a pioneer, an innovator, and something of a combination of prophet, martyr and fanatic. Henry Evelyn Bliss summed him up thus: 'He had a mind of large ideas, and of "dreams" that became ideas, and ideas that he made realities. He was a born reformer, in the better sense, and an idealist, an optimist too. He became an influential educator, an effectual advocate, a promoter of undertakings, and a doughty defender.' (35)

It will be clear from the foregoing account that Dewey's career as a librarian was guided by those same principles that guided the careers of the other great librarians. The connection with education—the librarian as an educated person, and as an educator—has been sufficiently dwelt on; Dewey's apprenticeship as a librarian was plainly served at Amherst; he dedicated himself completely to the integration of the librarian's role into the prevailing social and political system; and without doubt the libraries at Amherst and Columbia (particularly the latter) grew under his care.

Now, of course, it cannot be concluded that the adoption of these principles by any librarian will make him or her an Edwards, a Panizzi or a Dewey. On the basis of historical evidence such principles (and no others) will certainly guarantee an effective fulfilment of the role of librarian; but to become an Edwards, a Panizzi or a Dewey would require a total and self-sacrificing commitment, along with the possession of quite exceptional personal attributes.

Indeed the resemblances, both trivial and profound, between these three great librarians are very striking. All, for example, prosecuted their public crusades to the detriment of their private lives. All of them, of necessity, were pugnacious, quarrelsome and impatient. All of them worked inordinately hard. All of them were—as Fremont Rider wrote of Dewey—basically the same mixture of pioneer, crusader, prophet, fanatic and—unfortunately—martyr.

References
1 JOHNSON, E D: *History of libraries in the Western world*, 2nd ed, 1970.
2 THOMPSON, J W: *Ancient libraries*, 1940.
3 PARSONS, E A: *The Alexandrian Library*, 1952.
4 PARSONS, E A: *op cit*, 3.
5 PARSONS, E A: *op cit*, 3.
6 THOMPSON, J W: *op cit*, 2.
7 JOHNSON, E D: *op cit*, 1.
8 CLARK, J W: *The care of books*, 1901.
9 THORNTON, J L: *The chronology of librarianship*, 1941.
10 BLISS, H E: *The organization of knowledge in libraries and the subject approach to books*, 2nd ed, 1939.

11 KELLY, T: *A history of public libraries in Great Britain, 1845-1965*, 1973.

12 Quoted in THOMPSON, C S: *Evolution of the American public library 1653-1876*, 1952.

13 Quoted in KELLY, T: *op cit*, 11.

14 Quoted in KELLY, T: *op cit*, 11.

15 BOSTWICK, A E: *The American public library*, 1910.

16 Quoted in KELLY, T: *op cit*, 11.

17 BOSTWICK, A E: *op cit*, 15.

18 KELLY, T: *op cit*, 11.

19 WARD, P L: *Women and librarianship in 1975. Library Association record*, 77(4) April 1975, 82-83.

20 SCHILLER, A: *Women in librarianship. Advances in librarianship*, 4, 1974.

21 KENYON, Sir F: *Libraries and museums*, 1930.

22 JOHNSON, E D: *op cit*, 1.

23 IRWIN, R: *The origins of the English library*, 1958.

24 SAYERS, W C B: *A manual of classification for librarians and bibliographers*, 3rd ed, 1955.

25 RIDER, F: *The scholar and the future of the research library*, 1944.

26 GOODRUM, C A: *The Library of Congress*, 1974.

27 MUNFORD, W A: *Edward Edwards*, 1963.

28 GREENWOOD, T: *Edward Edwards*, 1902.

29 COWTAN, R: *A biographical sketch of Sir Anthony Panizzi*, 1873.

30 MILLER, E: *Prince of librarians*, 1967.

31 MILLER, E: *op cit*, 30.

32 MUNFORD, W A: *op cit*, 27.

33 MILLER, E: *op cit*, 30. .

34 RIDER, F: *Melvil Dewey*, 1944.

35 BLISS, H E: *op cit*, 10.

CHAPTER SEVEN

The classifcation and cataloguing of libraries

1 ORIGINS

'Be the collection of Books whatever, were it of fifty thousand Volumes,' wrote Gabriel Naudé in the seventeenth century, 'it would no more merit the name of a Library, than an assembly of thirty thousand men the name of an army, unless they be martially in their several quarters, under the conduct of their Chiefs and Captains.' (1)

This is a vivid formulation of the very first principle relating to the classification and cataloguing of libraries: namely, that a library must be arranged in some kind of order. Library history also indicates that not only should a library be arranged in order, but that a list of its contents should be provided.

In his account of ancient libraries, James Westfall Thompson tells us (2) that at Edfu in Egypt, the library building known as the 'House of Papyrus' had its catalogue of priestly books engraved on its walls. The catalogue comprised two registers, the first covering twelve coffers of works, the second twenty-two. There is evidence of a classification, for the second register is concerned with works on magic. Thompson also records that in the clay tablet libraries of Babylonia and Assyria the tablets were numbered in different series according to their places in the library. For the purposes of identifying the location of each tablet, every series was named from the words or sentence which headed the

139

first tablet, and each succeeding tablet had its proper number: such as, 'Sixteenth tablet of the evil spirits'. And to ensure correct sequence, a line was drawn at the end of the inscription on each tablet, and the first line of the tablet next in the series was written after it.

The tens of thousands of clay tablets were arranged on shelves for easy consultation, and were furnished with lists of titles or catalogues. Many tablets had a colophon, giving the tablet's place in its series, the name of the writer, and often a date. In the Kalakh collection, under the direction of a librarian called Nabu-zuqub-gina (who was in charge from the sixth year of Sargon, 716BC, to the twenty-second year of Sennacherib, 684BC), the catalogue entries included the title of the work, the number of lines, the contents, the *incipit* or opening words (which also served as the title), and each of its important parts or subdivisions. 'Books,' concludes Thompson, echoing Naudé, 'do not make a library until they have been arranged in some sort of order. Hence the formation of a catalogue.'

Ashurbanipal's library was also classified and catalogued. According to the account of it given by Elmer D Johnson, (3) the library was kept in many rooms in the king's palace, and there was apparently some subject arrangement by rooms. One room, for example, was devoted to tablets relating to history and government, another to those concerning legends and mythology, and so on. The clay tablets themselves were kept in earthen jars, and the jars housed in rows on shelves. Each tablet bore an identification label which indicated the jar, shelf and room in which it was to be found. Inside the door of each room, on the walls, was a list of the works held in that room: a kind of shelf-list, in fact. Also in each room, again near the door, were tablets which approximated to a subject catalogue or descriptive bibliography. The entries on such tablets gave the titles of works, the number of tablets for each work, the number of lines, opening words, important subdivisions, and a location or classification symbol. Some of these catalogue tablets which have survived are in a worn condition, showing that they were well used.

From this account, another principle emerges, relating to the kind of arrangement which has been most frequently adopted by libraries for some twenty-five centuries: namely, that libraries are most effectively arranged according to subject. This is patently logical, for since libraries are storehouses of knowledge, it follows that they should be arranged according to subject.

It is also interesting to note that the identification of an item in Ashurbanipal's library did not depend on (or even include) the author's name. As D M Norris pointed out, (4) ancient catalogues were classified subject catalogues; if author catalogues were compiled, there is no trace left of them.

According to Norris also, the first real catalogue of any library was that of the Alexandrian Library made by Callimachus. The identity of Callimachus is not certain, but he is usually supposed to be the Alexandrian poet who flourished between 310 and 240 BC. Callimachus prepared a classified catalogue—probably as an individual enterprise rather than an institutional effort of the Alexandrian Library itself, in the view of James Westfall Thompson—which was arranged in one hundred and twenty classes. The catalogue was made on slips of paper called Penakes, and on each slip was written a short title which corresponded exactly with the label on the appropriate papyrus roll. Norris gives as a 'rough plan' of the main divisions of the catalogue, the following:

1) Epic writers, 2) Dramatic writers, 3) Writers on law,
4) Philosophical writers, 5) Historical writers,
6) Oratorical works, 7) Rhetorical works, and
8) Miscellaneous works.

These divisions, she says, were further subdivided, and under the subdivisions, the entries were arranged alphabetically by the names of the authors, or else chronologically. Callimachus, it seems, provided in each entry in his catalogue the title of the work, the first line, and a biographical note of the author; in some cases, he gave a brief analysis of the work itself. Thus, as Norris observes, the year 240BC saw the production of a library catalogue which was a classified catalogue, a bibliography and a biographical dictionary all in one.

141

Edward Alexander Parsons, the most notable historian of the Alexandrian Library, reminds us, (5) however, that our knowledge of Callimachus's subject divisions is largely conjectural. He himself suggests that there were ten divisions, as opposed to Norris's eight: he does not include her 'Rhetorical works', but does introduce three other classes: Medicine, Mathematical science, and Natural science. Elmer D Johnson (6) accepts, in common with Norris and Parsons, the classes of Oratory, History, Laws, Philosophy, and Miscellany; of the remaining three, one, Medicine, fits in with Parson's view, while the remaining two he describes as Lyric Poetry and Tragedy. James Westfall Thompson (7) (since Callimachus's famous work is lost) will accept evidence only of five main classes, which he lists as follows: 1) Poetry, 2) History, 3) Philosophy, 4) Oratory, and 5) Miscellaneous.

It is however sufficient to know with reasonable certainty that the Alexandrian Library was arranged by subject. H L Pinner believes (8) that the origins of its arrangement lay in the way in which Aristotle ordered his private library: 'The Library of Aristotle was not only remarkable for its extent; it was also the first library to be designed and arranged on a definite plan. It became the example upon which the great libraries of Alexandria were later constructed. It is difficult to imagine how Aristotle could have written what he did without the continuous use of a scientifically ordered library, for his works included every branch of knowledge known at the time.' Parsons hints at another historical link in noting that Assyrian enthusiasts believe that Nineveh was the forerunner of the Alexandrian, and that Callimachus followed the 'technical library rules' found in the library of Ashurbanipal.

The picture which Parsons presents of the Alexandrian Library is certainly an impressive one. He visualises the arrangements as follows: 'Here in ten great Halls, whose ample walls were lined with spacious *armaria*, numbered and titled, were housed the myriad manuscripts containing the wisdom, knowledge, and information, accumulated by the genius of the Hellenic peoples. Each of the ten Halls was assigned to a separate department of learning . . . the Halls were used by scholars for general research, althoug there were smaller separate rooms for individuals or groups in special studies.'

2 THE MEDIAEVAL PERIOD

The principle that libraries should be arranged according to subject continued to be in evidence during the Middle Ages. Johnson notes (9) that if the size of a mediaeval library warranted it, the books were broadly classified by subject, and sometimes by size or acquisition. Theological books might be grouped separately from secular works; Latin works from works in other languages; textbooks from more advanced treatises. The religious works might be subdivided into further categories—scriptures, commentaries, bibliographies, service books; and the secular works might be arranged according to the *trivium* and *quadrivium*, the mediaeval teaching curriculum (the former comprising grammar, logic and rhetoric, and the latter, arithmetic, geometry, music and astronomy). The university library of the Sorbonne in the late thirteenth century, for example, was arranged in major subject divisions, including those of the *trivium* and *quadrivium*, plus theology, medicine and law.

Johnson also notes that in some libraries the various subject divisions were designated by letters and these letters were prominently inscribed on the bookchests. John Willis Clark refers (10) to a description of the system employed by the Benedictine Priory of St Martin at Dover, given in a catalogue made in 1389 by John Whytfeld. The library there was divided into nine classes (Distinctions), marked according to the first nine letters of the alphabet. Each of the nine classes was divided into seven shelves (grades), numbered I to VII from the bottom shelf up. To such class-letters, an arabic figure was added to show the position each book occupied in the order of placing on the shelf concerned.

Johnson adds that in early university libraries not only were the books shelved roughly by subject, but that at the end of a shelf there was usually a list of the books shelved there. He observes that though there were some local classification schemes, these (like that of the Benedictine Priory at Dover) commonly amounted to no more than location symbols referring to desk, shelf and book number. Such broad classification systems were adequate enough until the collections began to grow; but later in the mediaeval period more complex schemes began to be formulated. The subsequent development of classification schemes will be examined in the next section of the present chapter.

Catalogues of mediaeval libraries were made from the earliest times, and examples survive from the eighth century onwards. N R Ker prefaces his survey (11) of the extant books from the mediaeval libraries of Great Britain by commenting that the primitive stage of such catalogues was of short titles and arrangement roughly by subject, without any means of identifying a particular book from the catalogue description. He cites in illustration the oldest catalogues of Durham and Lincoln, the Bury and Reading catalogues, the Glastonbury catalogue and the second Rochester catalogue (1202AD). He records that the late twelfth-century catalogue of Christ Church (Canterbury) is the first to give reference letters, which, by corresponding to letters entered in the books themselves, act as a means of certain identification. Then he remarks on the various improvements shown in the library catalogues of the thirteenth and fourteenth centuries: books grouped by donors; the recording of opening words; arrangement according to the actual arrangement of the books on the shelves and recording the several presses or shelves; and the recording of press-marks. He concludes by noting that the earliest considerable catalogues to record the opening words of the second leaf of each book (*secundo folio*) are those of Dover (1389) and Durham (1391): a method of distinguishing books which became almost universal.

D M Norris, in her history of cataloguing and cataloguing methods, (12) furnishes a more complete description of mediaeval library catalogues on the basis of a detailed examination of a number of outstanding examples. A mediaeval catalogue of the period 1100-1200 (for example, that of Durham Cathedral Library of 1162) consisted of brief entries ('Bucolica et Georgica Vergilii' is a typical example), roughly grouped by subject, on parchment pages each with two columns. The entries in the Durham catalogue run on in paragraphs, with gaps for (presumably) additions, the end of each entry being signalled only by a full-stop.

Norris then turns to the period 1200-1300, and examines the catalogue of Glastonbury Abbey Library (1247), the *Registrum Librorum Angliae* (1250-1296), and the *Tabulae Septem Custodiarum super Bibliam*. The first of these is of interest because in it, if a book was a real contribution to its subject but its author was not well known, then the book is classed under its subject; however, if the author was famous, then the book appears under his name and there is no entry under subject. The *Registrum* is a union list of the holdings of 183 monastic establishments; each entry consists only of the title of the work, with a list of locations (represented by numbers). The *Registrum* is therefore in contrast to earlier catalogues, which were only concerned with listing and identifying the holdings of one particular library; it is indeed the earliest example of cooperative cataloguing. The *Tabulae Septem* is a union list also, covering some 80 authors, arranged in alphabetical order; as Norris observes, until then, 'such an order seems to be unknown'.

Of the catalogues of the next period, 1300-1400, Norris notes that on the whole a subject arrangement continues to be favoured; a new feature is that some have a method of press-marking; and alphabetical order is not in common use. In the period 1400-1500, collegiate and cathedral catalogues are in the majority, with monastic catalogues falling into second place; and again, subject arrangement is still preferred.

In Norris's view, the fifteenth century marks a definite break in the history of cataloguing. With the sixteenth century came the idea that some system was needed in the making of catalogues. In mediaeval cataloguing, books were listed more as an inventory of property, rather than—as in modern times—a key to the library. The further development of cataloguing from the sixteenth century onwards will be treated in the final section of the present chapter.

3 THE DEVELOPMENT OF MODERN CLASSIFICATION SYSTEMS

Some account has already been given of the classification of Ashurbanipal's library, of the Alexandrian Library, and of mediaeval libraries. The classification devised in the sixteenth century by Konrad Gesner (1516-1565) has been described by W C Berwick Sayers (13) as an interlude between ancient and modern.

Gesner began publishing his *Bibliotheca universalis* in 1545, in three parts. The first part was an alphabetical author list of all books in Latin, Greek and Hebrew, with titles, subjects and annotations. The second part, *Pandectarum sive partitionum universalum* (1548-9), was a systematically classified arrangement of all the books catalogued in the first part. The third part was to have been an alphabetical subject-catalogue of the books in the second part, but Gesner ultimately contented himself with a subject-index only.

Gesner's classification in the second part of his work is based on the mediaeval enumeration of studies noted in the previous section, the *trivium* and *quadrivium*. Sayers therefore characterises the scheme as one which follows 'the order in which the successive studies in a university were pursued'.

The identical principle lay behind the classification of the Bodleian Library when it was first opened in 1602. The library was divided into four subject groups or Faculties: Theology, Law, Medicine and Arts. In 1604, Bodley wrote to his Librarian, Thomas James, recommending that Law should take precedence over Medicine; but when the first catalogue was published in 1605, the order had been changed to Theology, Medicine, Law and Arts. The books were divided by size; the folios were chained to desks, and the quartos and octavos kept under lock and key. Within the subject classes, the books were arranged on the shelves in alphabetical order of surname.

A few decades later, in 1643, Gabriel Naudé published his *Bibliothecae Cordesianae catalogus*. This was the catalogue of the considerable library collected originally by Jean de Cordes but subsequently acquired by Cardinal Mazarin (for whom Naudé was Librarian). Naudé used the following classification in his catalogue: Theology, Medicine, Bibliography, Chronology, Geography, History, Military Art, Jurisprudence, Council and Canon Law, Philosophy, Politics, and Literature.

Edward Edwards (14) cites this scheme with obvious approval, remarking that Naudé 'disclaimed all desire to achieve reputation as a daring innovator'. Edwards had no time for 'far-fetched schemes' by 'super-subtle writers'. Naudé himself wrote (15) that for a classification scheme he favoured the 'most facil, the least intricate, most natural practified, and which follows the Faculties of Theology, Physick, Jurisprudence, Mathematicks, Humanity, and others, which should be subdivided each of them into particulars, according to their several members, which for this purpose ought to be reasonably well understood by him who has charge of the Library'.

The schemes of Gesner, the Bodleian, and Naudé, all point —as did the schemes used at Nineveh and in the Alexandrian Library—to the formulation on an historical basis of a further principle of librarianship: namely, that practical convenience should dictate how subjects are to be grouped in a library.

This principle was equally apparent in the so-called 'French system' of classification which, according to Sayers, (16) had its origins in the schemes of Jean Garnier (1678), Ismael Bouilliau (1679), Gabriel Martin (1705) and Guillaume de Bure (1763), and which reached its apotheosis when Jacques-Charles Brunet expanded it to form the basis of the arrangement for the classified part (vol 6) of his *Manuel du libraire et d'amateur de livres* (Paris, 1810). Brunet's main headings were: Theology, Jurisprudence, Science and Arts, Belles-lettres, and History. Such groupings were not philosophically-based but were ones which were found to be, in Sayers's own words, 'practically convenient'.

Various other nineteenth-century schemes were derived from Brunet's classification: for instance, that proposed by Thomas Hartwell Horne for the British Museum (*Outlines for the classification of a library, submitted to the Trustees of the British Museum*, London, 1825); and Edward Edwards's scheme for a Town Library proposed in his *Memoirs of libraries* (1859). The British Museum scheme, dating from about 1836-8, is (in Sayer's words) 'more nearly related to the French system than to any other'.

In his *Memoirs of libraries* Edward Edwards examines the 'French system' as well as more elaborate schemes such as that devised at the beginning of the nineteenth century by one Girault of Auxonne (a scheme which in Edwards's opinion showed the 'plentiful crop of practical absurdities' which can grow out of a 'supersubtle theory'), and it is very apparent that he approves the hospitality and simplicity of the former type of scheme and thoroughly condemns the latter type—noting that even so 'not a little both of time and ingenuity is still misdirected with similar perversity'.

Edwards fully accepted the principle that a library must be arranged in some kind of order, and that that order had to be according to subject. He remarks that for a librarian to say that he prefers not to classify his books is like a sculptor saying 'that, for his part, he thought marble was seen to most advantage in the block'. To Edwards's way of thinking, all schemes for the classification of libraries fall into one of two groups, 'the first group claiming a scientific genesis, and seeking a philosophical precision; the other content with the more modest pretensions of rendering service in the separation of things that plainly differ, and in the facilitation of our daily tasks'. Thus he can praise Francis Bacon's classification of human knowledge (in *The advancement of learning*, 1605), but see it nevertheless as being 'far better adapted to the purposes of the Historian of Learning and of the Sciences than to those of the Librarian'. In sum, Edwards also subscribed to the principle that subjects should be grouped in a library according to practical convenience. He did observe, however, that 'it is certain that a good catalogue will require a much more minute classification than would be either useful or practicable in the presses of a Library'.

Edwards's own scheme, for a Town Library, had only six main classes: I Theology; II Philosophy; III History; IV Politics and Commerce; V Sciences and Arts; and VI Literature and Polygraphy. Classification in the early days of public libraries in Great Britain (as recounted by Thomas Kelly) (17) was always very simple, and usually based on not more than a dozen main groupings. The groupings invariably began with Theology—a tradition going back of course to the mediaeval monasteries: indeed the early public libraries were merely continuing a system which had been handed down to them through subscription libraries and the libraries of mechanics' institutes and similar bodies. Just how strong the tradition of making Theology the first subject-division is evidenced by the fact that as late as 1877 Richard Garnett in his paper *On the system of classifying books on the shelves followed at the British Museum* (in the *Transactions of the International Conference of Librarians* of that year) declared that, as in the British Museum scheme, all classification schemes should follow this practice.

The year 1876 was a landmark in the history of library classifications, for it saw ·the publication of Melvil Dewey's Decimal Classification. In Dewey's scheme was manifest the three principles of librarianship relating to classification which have been formulated so far in this historical survey: first, that a library must be arranged in some kind of order; second, that that order should be according to subject; and third, that practical convenience should dictate how the subjects should be grouped. The title of Dewey's work (published anonymously) was *A classification and subject index for cataloguing and arranging the books and pamphlets of a library*; the first edition consisted of twelve pages of tables, and eighteen pages of index—forty-two in all. After nine years (in 1885) a greatly-expanded second edition appeared, in 486 pages.

Dewey's scheme has only nine main classes, excluding General Works (000)—Philosophy (100), Religion (200), Social Science (300), Language (400), Pure Science (500), Technology (600), Arts (700), Literature (800), and History (900). These nine classes, 100-900, are subdivided again 1-9, and then a third time 1-9; and then decimally 1-9, indefinitely if required. Thus 500 is Science; 510 is Mathematics; 512 is Algebra; and 512.2 is Algebraic equations. The scheme uses many mnemonic devices in its various subdivisions—for example, in geographical division wherever it occurs, there is a regular and familiar pattern of digits.

Apart from the simplicity of its main subject divisions, and apart from its good notation, the scheme also had to offer the practical convenience of an index. Dewey himself considered that his 'relative subject index' was 'the most important feature of the system', and his most original contribution to library classification. 'Relative,' explains Sayers, 'merely means that each subject which is indexed is shown in its relation to a larger subject (or class or division) or after the entry word the phase of the subject is indicated.' And Henry Evelyn Bliss comments: (18) '. . . it was so obvious a necessity. Books, even those with systematic contents, had from time immemorial been indexed. Why then should not a subject-catalog, or a classification, be indexed?'

Sayers makes some attempt to trace the provenance of various features of Dewey's scheme. He recounts how Dewey studied intensively for six months all the classification schemes that were in vogue in his day, and 'received suggestions' in particular from the schemes of Natale Battezzati (*Nuovo sistema de catalogo bibliografico generale*, a variant of Brunet), W T Harris, and Jacob Schwartz. According to Sayers, Dewey copied most from W T Harris, an American philosopher and educationalist, 'who devised his inversion and expansion of Bacon's intellectual chart in 1870 for the

150

arrangement of his catalogue of the St. Louis Public School Library'. Bacon's chart (1605) was based on the mental faculties of Memory (History), Imagination (Poesy) and Reason (Philosophy). But, as Sayers adds, 'While Bacon and his successors determined the curious outline, the internal order is really that which subjects were studied in 1876 in a particular college'. In other words, the grouping of the subjects by Dewey was dictated by practical convenience; indeed, Sayers also records that the working out of the individual classes was done for Dewey in the first instance by the faculties of Amherst College.

As for the decimal notation, Sayers notes that a decimal numbering system for a library was devised as early as 1583, by Lacroix du Maine for Henry II of France. But this system numbered the shelves decimally, not the books; as did also Nathaniel Shurtleff's *A decimal system for the arrangement and administration of libraries* (Boston, 1856).

Sayers concedes though, despite his attempts at seeking provenance for Dewey's scheme, that the aim of the Decimal Classification was purely practical; and he reports that Dewey himself described his system as a series of pigeon-holes into which material might be fitted—even declaring that it mattered less in what pigeon-hole a book was fitted than that all books on the same subject should be in the same pigeon-hole, and that that pigeon-hole should be indexed. Dewey in fact regarded his system as one for classifying nine special libraries. The effect therefore is that of nine special classifications conjoined. Such order as there is derives, as has been noted, from Harris's inversion of Bacon's intellectual chart— hence the otherwise inexplicable separation of Language from Literature, and Social Science from History. It is curious to reflect (and this essential point entirely escapes Sayers) that these blemishes on the practical convenience of the Dewey system arise entirely from his minor and uncharacteristic dalliance with a philosophical basis for a library classification. Sayers concludes by saying that the great practical strengths of Dewey's scheme are that it is

151

hospitable, flexible, has a splendid notation, and has been kept revised.

In praise of Dewey, it is also worth recalling Edward Edwards's prescription (19) for a good library classification: not, he wrote, 'logical concatenation, subtle analysis, or striking terminology', but 'simplicity, clear definition, and (as far as may be practicable) familiar and time-honoured names'. Dewey's scheme surely meets these criteria; and indeed we know that Dewey was familiar with, and an admirer of, Edwards's writings.

Bliss also observes (20) that 'Dewey was intent on practical convenience rather than logical order', and explains the success of the Decimal Classification fairly and succinctly thus: 'The Decimal Classification . . . filled a real need in the hundreds of public libraries that were springing up everywhere in this country. The comparative simplicity of its notation for its thousand subjects and the convenience of its index commended it; and there was no better system at hand. These considerations account for the remarkable success that attended its progress.'

Dewey's biographer, Fremont Rider, (21) considered that the scheme's best feature was its 'easily grasped simplicity'; and that what also recommended it were its ever-expandable base and its 'relative' method of book arrangement (as opposed to the up till then almost universal system of 'fixed location').

But the proof of the pudding is in the eating; and what really endorses the practical merits of Dewey's scheme is the fact—supplied by Rider—that by 1927 his classification system was in use in 96 per cent of all public libraries in the United States, and in 89 per cent of college and university libraries.

To return, however, to the nineteenth century. The year 1891 saw the development by Charles Ammi Cutter in America of his Expansive Classification. Again this was of (in Sayers's phrase) 'the inverted Baconian order', its basic classes being Philosophy, History, Science and Art. The classification consisted of separate sets of tables, covering the whole field of knowledge. The first was very broad and suitable only for small collections; the second was subdivided at greater length; the third at still greater length; and so on, until the seventh, which was according to Cutter full enough and minute enough for a library the size of the British Museum Library. The order of the classes was declared by Cutter to be 'evolutionary': that is, in the natural sciences, the parts of each subject appear in the order which that theory assigns to their appearance in creation. Cutter's notation is alphabetical, alphabetically divided (theoretically, ad infinitum). The Seventh Expansion of the scheme was in progress when Cutter died; and though the work was contined by experts under the general editorship of Cutter's nephew, W P Cutter, it has not been maintained.

In the United Kingdom, meanwhile, the first public library to adopt the Dewey classification system was Ashton under Lyme, which opened in 1881 and which published a catalogue based on Dewey in 1883—six years after Dewey had described his system at the first conference of librarians in Britain in 1877.

From the 1890s, as Kelly recounts, (22) open access began to be put into practice in an increasing number of British public libraries. Previously, with closed access, the arrangement of the catalogue was the all-important thing, and the actual order of the books on the shelves did not matter so long as each had a number linking it with the catalogue. However, once readers were admitted to the shelves, it was necessary to arrange the books in such a way that the reader could find his way about without constant reference to the catalogue or to an assistant. Hence there arose the need for a shelf classification.

At Clerkenwell, James Duff Brown, as one of the pioneers of the open access system, devised (in 1895) the Quinn-Brown classification (compiling it in collaboration with J H Quinn, the Librarian of Chelsea). This subsequently became the Adjustable Classification (1898), and finally, in its fully developed form, the Subject Classification (1906). Brown aimed to arrange the various branches of knowledge in some kind of logical order, in his case based on a concept of historical evolution—Matter, Force, Life, Mind, and Record. The notation he used was of a mixed kind: the main classes distinguished by letters of the alphabet, the sub-divisions by numerals. Thus, after a Generalia class (A), came B-D Physical Science (representing Matter and Force), and subsequently, J-K Philosophy and Religion and L Social and Political Science (representing Mind). Sayers notes that Brown's theory that every art springs from some definite cause produced results such as Sound leading up to Music, and Light up to Optics: excellent examples of sense and practical convenience being sacrificed at the altar of philosophy.

Brown's system was adopted in more than a score of British libraries. However, the future of library classification in the United Kingdom lay, as in the United States, with the Dewey Decimal Classification. In 1937, 380 public libraries in Great Britain used Dewey or modifications of Dewey, and only 34 used the Adjustable or Subject Classification. Now, in the 1970s Dewey is almost universal.

The beginning of the twentieth century witnessed the inception of what Sayers refers to as 'the greatest and most modern of utilitarian schemes', the Library of Congress classification scheme. The scheme is an entirely practical one, devised from a comparison of existing schemes and taking into consideration the particular conditions of the Library, the character of its collections and their probable use. As Sayers comments, 'the Library of Congress scheme has grown from actual work in a cataloguing room'. Herbert Putnam, appointed Librarian of Congress in 1899, himself wrote' 'The system has not sought to follow strictly the scientific order of subjects. It has sought rather convenient sequence of the various groups, considering them as groups of books, not as groups of mere subjects.' Additionally, in his *Report and manual* of the Library of Congress for 1901, Putnam describes the function of a classifier in a library to be to arrange the books on the shelves in an orderly sequence; and declared that in a library which is to be used and which is to grow, the arrangement has to be not only orderly, but systematic and expandable, bringing together books on the same subject.

It will be seen therefore that the Library of Congress scheme, like Dewey's, is firmly anchored to the three historic first principles of library classification: that a library should be arranged in order; that the order should be of subject; and that the grouping of books by subject should be dictated by practical convenience.

The scheme itself was built up by a corps of classifiers, each a specialist in his subject. Each specialist worked over the books in his speciality and arranged them first in 'what appeared to be their most practical groups' (Sayers's phrase), the most important factor being the way in which people asked for books or made use of them. Each group was then divided into its component subjects as minutely as possible.

The outline of the scheme was drawn up in 1901, but took some forty more years to reach approximate completion. Cutter's Expansive Classification had the most influence on the outline, according to Sayers, though he adds that even so it has 'no recognizable natural or philosophical order'. The outline is as follows: A General works, B Philosophy and Religion, C History: Auxiliary Sciences, D History: General and Old World, E-F History: America, G Geography, H Social Sciences, J Political Science, K Law, L Education, M Music, N Fine Arts, P Philosophy and Literature, Q Science, R Medicine, S Agriculture, T Technology, U Military Science, V Naval Science, Z Bibliography and Library Science. For sub-division, the notation used is normally a second letter of the alphabet and then numerals. The general disposition of the main classes shows clearly the requirements of a library used by a legislature—the emphasis on historical, social and judicial sciences, on the country itself, on military and naval matters, and on agriculture. Each class was published as a separate volume, and has a separate index. Like the Dewey Classification, the scheme is basically a series of special classifications.

155

Four years after the inception of the Library of Congress scheme there was published, in 1905, the Universal Decimal Classification. This was the outcome of an international conference held in Brussels in 1895, which initiated a scheme, based on Dewey, for a comprehensive classifed index to published information. It has been described as an extended Dewey, permitting the sub-division of the main class numbers in the minutest detail for use in classifying information for special purposes, with the addition of devices to accommodate various aspects, forms and combinations of subjects. A second edition of the scheme was published in four volumes in 1927-33. The Universal Decimal Classification, like its parent scheme, and for the same reasons of practical convenience, has come to be widely used.

In 1929, an American librarian, Henry Evelyn Bliss, published a philosophical examination of library classification, *The organization of knowledge and the system of the sciences.* Bliss's argument is summed up as follows in John Dewey's introduction to the book: 'The reader learns to understand, as he follows the thought of Mr Bliss, that a library is not a mere depository of books, and that a merely arbitrary classification does not satisfy even the practical needs. A classification of books to be effective on the practical side must correspond to the relationships of subject matters, and this correspondence can be secured only as the intellectual, or conceptual, organization is based upon the order inherent in the fields of knowledge, which in turn mirrors the order of nature. The library serves a practical end, but it serves it best when practical tools and instrumentalities agree with the intrinsic logic of subjects, which corresponds to natural realities. The right organization of knowledge in libraries embodies, moreover, a record of attained unification of knowledge and experience, while it also provides an indispensable means to the development of further knowledge.'

Historically, of course, Bliss's basic argument that a library classification should be tied to a knowledge classification goes back a very long way. Sayers observed that there is a

whole school of librarians who consider that 'a library classification is merely a philosophical classification with certain
added classes and apparatus, form classes, notations and
indexes'; (23) and notes a number of early thinkers who
created classifications of knowledge (also called philosophical
classifications, classifications of the sciences, or metaphysical
classifications). He traces the beginning of such systems back
to Plato and Aristotle; their continuation by such names as
Pliny (AD 23-27), Porphyry (c300), Bede (673-735), Alcuin
(736-804), Roger Bacon (1266) and Francis Bacon (1605);
and their modern counterparts in the work of Descartes
(1644), Bentham (1816), Hegel (1817), Comte (1822),
Herbert Spencer (1864), Karl Pearson (1900) and others.
Sayers concludes by stating that the argument for linking a
library classification with a knowledge classification is that
since the latter will include the sciences, books will therefore
be arranged in the order in which the scientist himself would
place them (though a problem will be that with every change
in the classification of a science, the corresponding classification of books would have to change—and this is not easy);
and he sums up the arguments against basing a library classification on a knowledge classification as follows: first, books
cannot be arranged in the same way as subjects; second, every
book is more complex than a single subject; third, knowledge
classifications can be too detailed and also can cover areas
where no literature exists; and fourth, the philosopher's aim
(to discover the relationship of things) is different from the
librarian's (to put books in the order in which readers use and
expect to find them).

A more powerful argument than any advanced in Sayers's
summary against basing library classifications on knowledge
classifications is to be found in the historical evidence presented even in the present short survey of the history of the
various schemes. Those which have been based on a philosophical approach have had little success; those which have
followed the principle that practical convenience should
dictate the order of subjects—for example, Brunet, the

Dewey Decimal Classification and the Library of Congress classification—have been more widely accepted and used, and have survived longer. Another point is that while Bliss's intellect and perception are not to be denied, it is a useful corrective to reflect that many who have firmly held the opposing view—for example, Naudé, Edwards, Dewey—were not his inferiors in the possession of these same attributes.

Bliss continued his study of library classification in a further book, *The organization of knowledge in libraries, and the subject-approach to books* (1933; 2nd ed, 1939). The work begins with some preliminary quotations from other writers on the subject: from Sayers, who came to believe that a book classification must be based on a classification of knowledge; from Charles Ammi Cutter, who thought that if the maker of a scheme for book arrangement kept a classification of knowledge in mind, the result would be more likely to have permanent value; and from Ernest Cushing Richardson, who considered that a scheme would be better, and last longer, for keeping to 'the true order of the sciences'.

Bliss's view is that we cannot settle down with the supposition that, in a changing world, the subject approach to books was solved in 1873 by an undergraduate (Dewey), or definitively in 1900 by an international institute (the Universal Decimal Classification), or by a national library (the Library of Congress classification). He refers to the notion that the problem of library classification is 'inherently and practically insoluble', saying that 'the historical situation' has been 'pervaded by a threadbare tradition and myopic conservatism or complacency'. And he sums up his interpretation of the history of classification as follows: 'In the history of the succession of arbitrary systems we have not found any consistent growth that deserves to be called a development. So there is less reason for grounding these introductory observations on the remoter past. In the system of knowledge, of the sciences, we did, however, find a development, relational and probably causal, and that it is of intellectual and critical value to survey it.'

He sees that the philosophical systems of Aristotle, Gesner and Bacon did 'somewhat influence' the library classifications of Callimachus, Bouilliau (antecedent to Brunet), Merlin, Harris and Dewey, but that 'practical convenience' was always a more significant factor. He cites the philosopher Leibnitz, of whose library system the first three classes—Theology, Jurisprudence and Medicine—were assigned to the principal university faculties; and he notes how the mediaeval division of studies, the *trivium* and *quadrivium*, permeated the systems, for example, of Naudé, Bouilliau (1678), Garnier (1678), Martin (1740), Brunet (1810) and Horne (1825). He continues: 'The purpose of organizing knowledge, or study, had not yet emerged. In the days of Brunet books were not classified on such principles. Theology should out of respect and from habit of thought come first; but it did not matter much whether History or Literature or Philosophy came last, or whether Arts preceded Sciences or not. Some librarians think the same on these matters today.'

Bliss's main thesis is that the fault of established systems of classification is that 'in the purpose to be practical in the particular historical and local situations, in the several libraries where they originated, they have disregarded the essential principles of classification for organization of knowledge'.

In answering Bliss's arguments, it is only necessary to begin by agreeing with him that there is no pattern of development in the history of library classifications, certainly not in the simplistic sense of some one system growing more defined and refined as the centuries have gone by. But what have emerged are the three principles, cited several times already in this chapter, governing the arrangement of libraries; and the last of these, relating to practical convenience, has achieved the status of being irrefutable. It has also emerged that what librarians have as a consequence sought, is a series of special subject classifications, the ordering of which classes has never been found to need any philosophical basis—only a practical one. The relation of library classifications to knowledge classifications has not been demonstrated to be a valid one historically.

159

In 1935, Bliss published his own scheme under the title *A system of bibliographic classification*; the full version appeared in four volumes, 1940-1957. His four main divisions are Philosophy, Science, History, Technologies and the Arts. He divides these into appropriate classes, placing side-by-side ('collocating') those classes which are most like in subject matter or interest. The result is that his sequence begins with philosophy, developing into science, then social sciences, history, geography, religion, politics, law, economics, technology, fine arts, language, literature, and bibliography. Alternative placings are catered for liberally.

Finally, in this historical survey of library classifications, mention must be made of the appearance in the twentieth century also of S R Ranganathan's Colon Classification. Ranganathan devised and developed this scheme in the 1920s, and it was first published in 1933. What made it different from previous schemes was its analytic and synthetic approach to classification, as opposed to the traditional enumerative approach. C D Batty has explained the underlying theory thus: (24) 'Almost all library classifications . . . were constructed according to a conventional pattern of classes divided into subclasses each of which was further divided, and the printed classification scheme was virtually the sole authority for the assignment of class numbers of books. If a topic was not named specifically in the scheme the librarian was compelled to find the nearest approximate place, so that the accuracy and helpfulness of class numbers depended on how recently the scheme had been revised, how wide and how deep was the knowledge of its inventor, and how closely the range and level of the stock of the library matched the preconceptions on which the scheme was based. . . .

'Dr Ranganathan saw how the principle of 'synthesis', of joining different terms together, could produce a far more useful and supple scheme than the old principle of identifying the required terms in a hierarchy of systematic subdivisions. He separated not only the general aspects that might occur with any specific subject, but also different aspects within the specific subjects themselves, and in doing so recognised that even among quite different specific subjects there were definable kinds of aspect that were repeated over and over again and could thus form the basis of a "synthetic" scheme.'

Ranganathan's scheme as such has had only a very limited success; indeed, J Mills noted in 1951 (25) that it then still had had no practical application in Great Britain, seventeen years after its first publication. Nevertheless, it has been claimed among other things that Ranganathan's theories underlie much if not most modern thought on classification and indexing (Batty); that his work has revitalised the whole study of classification (B I Palmer) (26); and that his approach recognizes the need 'for documentation service of the most exact and exhaustive kind' (Ranganathan himself) (27). Certainly it is true that Ranganathan's methods of analysis and synthesis have been widely used in the construction of special subject schemes, especially in the field of information retrieval. As far as the classification of the world's libraries, however, Ranganathan's work has not dislodged the established utilitarian schemes.

4 THE DEVELOPMENT OF MODERN CATALOGUING

It was noted in the first two sections of the present chapter that the earliest library catalogues were arranged by subject. The catalogue of one of the first libraries in the world (at Edfu in Egypt) was so arranged, as were those of the ancient libraries of Babylonia and Assyria, of Ashurbanipal's library, and of the Alexandrian Library. The same principle persisted into the mediaeval period.

It continued likewise into the age of the printed book. Aldus Manutius in 1498, for example, arranged his list of Greek books into Grammatica, Poetica, Logica, Philosophia and Sacra Scriptura; and Robert Estienne in 1546 similarly grouped the publications in his catalogue in various divisions such as Graeca, Grammatica, Historica and so on.

The sixteenth century also witnessed the appearance of Konrad Gesner's catalogue, described in the previous section. The first part of this catalogue, it will be recalled, was an alphabetical author list of all books in Latin, Greek and Hebrew, with titles, subjects and annotations. The second part, the *Pandectarum* (1548-9) was a systematically classified arrangement of the books catalogued in the first part. The third part was to be an alphabetical subject-catalogue of the books in the second part, but Gesner ultimately settled for a subject-index. Gesner suggested that librarians, instead of compiling author catalogues themselves, should use the catalogue for that purpose, inserting their own library's pressmarks against his entries for books.

In 1560, Florianus Treflerus, a Benedictine monk, published a work with the title *Methodus exhibens per varios indices, et classes subinde, quorumlibet librorum, cuiuslibet bibliothecae, breve, facilem, imitabilem ordinationem.* This recommended five catalogues for a library: an author catalogue, a classed catalogue in accordance with the arrangement of the books on the shelves, a subject index to all the books in the library, an alphabetical index to the last, and an index of books held in reserve stock. In the first of these five catalogues, each entry was to receive a shelf mark consisting of three letters—the first indicating size (eg P for Parvus), the second for colour (eg A for Albinus), and the third indicating the class (the classification running from A, Civil law, through to R, German writers).

Also in the sixteenth century, Andrew Maunsell, the bookseller, issued in 1595 the first part of a proposed three-part catalogue, listing books on divinity. The second part appeared in the same year, dealing with arithmetic, music, navigation and war. The third part, never issued, was to have covered the humanities—grammar, logic, rhetoric, law, history, poetry and 'policie'. Maunsell's rules for his catalogue were that it should be classed according to subject, with the entries arranged alphabetically under the author's surname; that anonymous works were to be entered under title or subject, and in some cases both; and that translations should be entered under author, translator, and subject.

Norris sums up the cataloguing history of the sixteenth century as follows: (28) 'With the close of the sixteenth

162

century, haphazard and individual methods of cataloguing began to vanish. Although the first code of rules did not appear until the next century, there is a vague realisation that some system is necessary, but what that system is, cannot yet be defined.'

Coming now to the seventeenth century, in 1605 appeared the catalogue of the Bodleian Library, a printed volume of 425 pages with 230 pages of appendix: a landmark in that this was the first general catalogue of a European library. Its compiler was the first Librarian of the Bodleian, Thomas James. Sir Thomas Bodley had insisted that the arrangement should be according to the four faculties—Theology, Medicine, Law and Arts—with an alphabetical order by author under each: as the catalogue itself stated, 'continet autem Libros Alphabetice dispositos secundum quatuor Facultates'. James himself did not like this arrangement, and the next catalogue of the Bodleian, published in 1620 was an alphabetical one, 'the first general library catalogue to be arranged in alphabetical order of the authors' names'. (Norris)

James's objection was to a classified library, not to a classified catalogue, and the 1605 catalogue, on Bodley's instructions, did no more than list each book as it stood on its shelf. James felt that the 1605 arrangement had to be abandoned, because he found so many books impossible to class correctly, and also because, through classifying, the works of one author were split up and scattered throughout the catalogue. James nevertheless spent much of his time during his retirement in making subject catalogues of the Bodleian, divided into main classes with sub-sections arranged alphabetically by heading, all with an alphabetical author index. The subjects he dealt with were Grammar, Geometry Astronomy, Architecture, Arithmetic, Optics, Cosmography, Geography, Chronology, Music, Logic, Military Arts, Moral Philosophy, Politics, Natural Philosophy, Rhetoric and History. This work was compiled about 1624-25 and published under the title *Synopsis subiectorum in singulis facultatibus authorumque qui de iis scripserunt*. Its value is shown by the fact that it was extensively used not only in the Bodleian but in all the college libraries.

This little piece of Bodleian history encapsulates a conflict which has dominated modern cataloguing: on the one hand, there is the need in a library for an accurate finding-list, an inventory; on the other is the principle, patently established over many centuries, as the present brief survey has shown, that a library must have a subject catalogue. The Bodleian needed a finding-list—hence the 1620 catalogue arranged straightforwardly by authors in alphabetical order; but as a library, as a store of knowledge, it required a subject key to that store.

Norris, as was noted at the end of the section of this chapter on the mediaeval period, characterises the seventeenth century generally as the time which saw the beginning of present-day cataloguing methods. In her view, such men as James, John Durie and Frederic de Rostgaard (1671-1745—a Dane who collected a considerable personal library and who drew up a cataloguing scheme as a consequence), gave particular consideration to the needs of students using libraries. In 1650 appeared the first dictionary catalogue—that is, author and subject entries in one sequence. This was the catalogue of the Library of Sion College, founded by the Reverend Thomas White (who died in 1632) for the use of all the clergy in London who were licensed to preach. This catalogue was however only a very rudimentary version of a dictionary catalogue. Books were given but one entry; if there was no author, then entry was under subject.

Printed catalogues were the rule in the seventeenth century; and press-marks were always included. These catalogues were kept up to date: for example, at the Bodleian, following the catalogues of 1605 and 1620, came a third one in 1674. Another feature of the period was the growing number of cataloguing codes.

Norris characterises the next century, the eighteenth, as a period 'well on the way towards the general uniformity of method of modern cataloguing'. Entries were brief, since catalogues continued to be printed; there was a tendency to make each entry fit one line of type. The eighteenth century also saw the appearance of the first national code of cataloguing rules, the French code of 1791. Norris also observes that of the eighteenth century catalogues she examined for her history of cataloguing, all were 'in the main, either author alphabetical or subject-classed', with author catalogues in the majority.

The nineteenth century was the most important and influential period in the history of modern cataloguing methods, just as it was in the history of classification systems. In Great Britain, developments in the British Museum Library, at the Bodleian, and in the newly-established public library system, were crucial.

The first catalogue of the British Museum Library was issued in two folio volumes in 1787, with the title *Librorum impressorum qui in Museo britannico adservantur catalogus*. It was compiled by Samuel Ayscough, Paul Henry Maty and Samuel Harper. A new edition, in seven volumes, appeared between 1813 and 1819, having been begun by Sir Henry Ellis and H H Baber in 1807, when the Trustees had decided that one alphabetical catalogue of all the separate collections should be made and that a general classed catalogue should also be compiled.

In 1826 the Trustees accepted a scheme for a classed catalogue. In the previous year, Thomas Hartwell Horne had presented to them his *Outlines for the classification of a library*, his aim being to 'make the Classed Catalogue of the British Museum—what no existing Catalogue of any Royal or National Library in Europe is—a standard work of perpetual reference'. (29)

Classed catalogues were common in this period, in plain evidence of the principle that a library must have a subject catalogue. Henry A Sharp cites a number of examples in his textbook on cataloguing. (30) There was the classified catalogue of the Signet Library, Edinburgh, compiled by its librarian, George Sandy, and issued in 1805; it had an alphabetical index of authors and subjects, and its arrangement was based on the classification of de Bure. In 1809 the Royal Institution of Great Britain published *A catalogue . . . methodically arranged, with an alphabetical index of authors*, compiled by William Harris. In 1812 the Surrey Institution published its catalogue, arranged by Horne's classification, with an author index. Horne himself, in 1827, produced a classed catalogue of the Library of Queen's College, Cambridge. A little later, between the years 1835 and 1852, the London Institution issued a 'systematically classed' catalogue in four volumes, arranged under class headings such as zoology (with sub-divisions), architecture, fine arts, and so on. Sharp notes that Edward Edwards considered this catalogue to be one of the best examples of its kind.

Sharp also observes that the preface to the London Institution catalogue 'contains a justification for the classified catalogue that makes interesting reading a hundred years later, if only because it may cause us to wonder how much, if at all, we have really progressed in our views on the functions of library catalogues'. The truth of the matter, of course, is that what has happened in the intervening hundred years is that a basic historically-established principle of librarianship—that a library must have a subject catalogue—has been neglected. Sharp goes on to quote usefully, as follows, from that preface: 'In concluding this preface with some remarks upon the subject of classification in catalogues, it will be scarcely requisite to notice the great and numerous advantages which a methodical arrangement of books possesses over a list that is simply alphabetical. With whatever accuracy the latter may be compiled, it can be effectually useful to those only who are in search of a particular work; or who are already well acquainted with authors in general, or at the least with such as have written upon the subject in which they are interested. Such a list, on the contrary, is of little benefit to the reader who is desirous of being informed what books are to be found in a large library upon any particular branch of knowledge; but a Classed Catalogue immediately furnishes

166

that information and exhibits, at the same time, the peculiar excellence of the collection. Nor is the answer that such an arrangement discovers the weakness of a public library, of sufficient importance to counteract the extensive utility of the plan; since the classes which most require improvement, are thus made known to such persons as might be both inclined and able to assist the establishment, if its peculiar deficiencies had been stated.

'The principle upon which a Classed Catalogue is constructed, is the division of the mass of human knowledge contained in printed books, into the most natural large and distinct heads; each being subdivided into such smaller sections as may comprise every variety of subject, at the same time that they are entirely independent of each other. The proper characteristics of such an arrangement, are a facility and a convenience of reference, and a simplicity of classification, in the number and distinctness of the chief departments and subdivisions: and in forming such a Catalogue the principle design is, to enable all who consult it readily to find either any particular *work*, or the *authors* upon any particular *subject*; as well as to furnish a clear view of the contents of the collection.'

Norris likewise records the multiplicity of classed catalogues in the period 1800-1850, but criticises them for the 'artificiality' of the classifications used. She observes in addition that it was the case with all of them that no systematic arrangement, either alphabetical by author, or chronological, is adopted under the various headings. This, together with the fact that their indexes referred only to page and not to the particular item, made them anything but quick and convenient to consult. Norris therefore remarks that it can be readily appreciated 'whence came the rooted objection of the latter half of the century to classed catalogues'. She also comments: 'Knowledge was neither scientifically nor logically divided; each librarian concocted a scheme to suit himself'. In conclusion on this topic, Norris notes that as a result of these difficulties, the dictionary form of catalogue was introduced as being simplicity itself compared to them.

To return, however, to the year 1826, to Thomas Hartwell Horne and the Trustees of the British Museum. Horne was engaged by the Trustees to compile a classed catalogue; but eight years and £7,000 later, the whole project was abandoned as a failure.

When a Select Committee of the House of Commons was set up in 1834 to enquire into the affairs of the Museum, it was informed that only two catalogues of the British Museum Library existed—the printed author catalogue of 1813-19, and the five-volume catalogue of the Library of George III. The committee soon became involved in a debate on the respective merits of author and classed catalogues, with Sir Henry Ellis, the Director of the Museum, supporting the former, and Edward Edwards speaking for the latter. In 1836, when the committee was still taking evidence on the cataloguing question, Panizzi was given the opportunity to express his views. 'The first and chief object of a catalogue,' he declared, 'is to give an easy access to the works which form part of the collection.' Panizzi favoured an alphabetically arranged author catalogue rather than a classed one, because in his opinion every classification scheme which had until that time been put forward was absurd, and because the continual discoveries in science made any classification ridiculous.

In the end, Panizzi had his way. Following his appointment as Keeper of the Printed Books in 1837, he insisted on the compilation of a new catalogue. He drew up a set of rules to govern the making of an author catalogue, and these were sanctioned by the Trustees in 1839. The rules themselves, ninety-one of them, were published in 1841, and constitute the first English cataloguing code. In the same year the first volume of the catalogue, containing letter A, was published. It was also the last volume to be published, because great difficulties were encountered (as Panizzi had foreseen) in letter-by-letter publication. The catalogue proceded, but in manuscript, because Panizzi did not like printed catalogues any more than he liked classed catalogues. It was in fact not until 1900 that a printed catalogue was issued.

The Bodleian Library, meanwhile, having issued a further catalogue in 1738, produced yet another in 1843. This last was much criticised, and it was decided that the Bodleian should adopt the British Museum rules drawn up by Panizzi. The British Museum was also to be imitated in that single titles were to be duplicated on slips of paper, and the slips mounted in alphabetical order; two copies of the catalogue were to be made up in this manner; and the remaining slips were to be sorted up into a classed catalogue. When finished in 1878, the catalogue consisted of 741 volumes; this was only the author catalogue; the classed catalogue was not started until that year.

The British Museum code of rules prevailed in the Bodleian until 1882, when E W B Nicholson, the then Librarian, drew up a set of 54 rules based on the code produced by the Library Association. The Compendious Catalogue Rules for the Author Catalogue of the Bodleian Library were issued in 1885, consisting of the 1882 rules with some additions, and were printed in 1893; a revised edition of them appeared in 1918, the number then having grown from 54 to 68.

The classed catalogue, started in 1878, came under strong attack in 1885 from a Professor H W Chandler, when the Librarian asked for more cataloguing staff. Norris quotes Chandler at length on the subject, as follows: 'Who tied the millstone of a classed catalogue round the Librarians neck, I do not know; but the classed catalogue & all the work that it entails is so much labour thrown away. No real scholar, no man who is capable of literary research, wants a classed catalogue; he hates the very sight of such a thing; it serves no useful purpose; it is a snare and a delusion. The sciolist, and he alone, thinks how delightful it would be to turn out any given subject and there see all the books that have been written on it. He does not know how impossible the thing is,

169

or what mischiefs result from the attempt to compass such a work. Most french catalogues are classed, and he who had had the ill luck, as I have, to consult them, retains a lively sense of detestation for those who were foolish enough to class the books. Could men of real knowledge be consulted, I am quite sure that a large majority, if not all, would infinitely prefer the alphabetical arrangement under authors names, to the best classed catalogue that could be devised.'

Nicholson's defence was simply that the value of the classed catalogue was sufficiently demonstrated by the use made of it.

Methods of cataloguing were also, of course, preoccupying the fledgling public libraries of this period. In the era 1845-1886, as Kelly recounts, (31) the users of public libraries enjoyed only 'indirect access': that is, they consulted the catalogues, not the shelves. The catalogue was invariably printed, and its preparation and revision was one of the major tasks of the librarian. The Parliamentary Committee of 1849, which was appointed to enquire into public libraries, referred to the necessity of providing catalogues, and declared that: 'So far as they have enquired, it appears to your committee that a catalogue, classified as to subjects, with an alphabetical list of authors, would be best'. (32)

Edward Edwards, as was mentioned earlier, favoured a classified subject catalogue, as opposed to an alphabetically arranged author catalogue. Most public libraries, though, including his own at Manchester, were content with mere class-lists, in alphabetical order of authors, following the main subject-divisions. Edwards began a detailed classified catalogue for the reference library at Manchester, but this was abandoned by his Library Committee as being too slow and too costly. Instead, Andrea Crestadoro produced a completely new catalogue, an author catalogue with author and subject index; and for branch lending libraries, he invented a catalogue known as an Index Catalogue, in which authors, titles and subjects were combined in a single alphabet. This was, in crude form, as Kelly notes, the type of catalogue which under the name of index or dictionary catalogue, soon became the most popular in all English public libraries. It was first used at the Hulme branch, Manchester, in 1867; J D Mullins's catalogue of the Birmingham Reference Library, in 1869, was of the same type; and further examples followed at Liverpool (1872), Rochdale (1873), Plymouth and Westminster (1877), and Newcastle upon Tyne (1880).

The spread of the public library movement in Great Britain and the United States, as H A Sharp observes, (33) created a public which wanted books about specific subjects just as much as by specific authors. Hence, in 1876, came the publication of Charles Ammi Cutter's *Rules for a dictionary catalogue*. Cutter did not invent the dictionary catalogue (whose history can be traced back to 1815 in the United States), but his rules still constitute the standard code. The first edition of his work contained 205 rules, the fourth (in 1904) contained 369. Cutter himself compiled the dictionary catalogue of the Boston Athenaeum, which appeared in five volumes between 1874 and 1882.

Earlier than Cutter's code had been the set of 39 cataloguing rules produced in 1852 by the Smithsonian Institution; these were on the lines of Panizzi's code. Both the American and British Library Associations each produced cataloguing codes before the end of the nineteenth century; eventually, in the twentieth century, they produced their first joint code, the *Cataloguing rules: author and title entries* (1908). This cooperation has continued between the two Associations, culminating in the *Anglo-American cataloguing rules* of 1967.

The end of the nineteenth century, and the beginning of the twentieth, saw the printed catalogue at its apogee. The British Museum catalogue completed at the turn of the century has already been mentioned. The London Library issued a one-volume catalogue, of 1,626 pages, in 1903, to be followed by eight annual supplements; in 1913-14, a new two-volume catalogue of 2,754 pages was issued, but the costs of printing and preparation of copy were high. Edinburgh University Library's three-volume catalogue was begun in 1899; printing started in 1915 but was not completed until 1923. The London and Edinburgh catalogues each covered some 400,000 volumes. The Bibliothèque Nationale started its *Catalogue générale des livres imprimés* in 1897, and reached authors whose name began with the letter I in 75 volumes: but as William Warner Bishop commented, (34) 'the cost in time and money of such an enterprise is too vast for any but a national treasury'.

In British public libraries, until the 1890s, printed dictionary catalogues held sway; but as the libraries grew in size, these catalogues became increasingly difficult and expensive to maintain. James Duff Brown, along with contemporaries such as Louis Stanley Jast, promoted class-lists; but by the turn of the century, card catalogues became more and more common. By the mid-1930s, the card or sheaf catalogue was standard practice in the municipal libraries.

The card catalogue, Kelly records, (35) was a technique adopted from business practice, and was introduced into Great Britain from the United States. Charles Ammi Cutter recommended its use at the first British conference of Librarians in 1877, and Newcastle upon Tyne Reference Library, opened in 1884, was entirely catalogued by this method.

William Warner Bishop, cited earlier, observes that though the card catalogue was a development of the nineteenth century, it was already known in France in the eighteenth century. Bishop is here referring to the French Code of 1791, mentioned briefly earlier in this section. After the French Revolution, the books of many private and institutional libraries became national property, and instructions were issued on the proper care of such collections. These instructions, addressed to custodians in all districts, consisted of rules for the formation of a card catalogue.

Bishop comments that the rapid spread and adoption of the card catalogue is one of the most significant features of modern library history. It was the only real alternative, in its time, to the printed catalogue: a fact pointed out as early as

1851 by Charles Coffin Jewett in his publication *A plan for stereotyping catalogues by separate titles, and for forming a general stereotyped catalogue of public libraries of the United States*. Bishop continues the story as follows: 'Efforts were made by the Library Bureau in the early nineties to make the supplying of printed catalog cards a commercial possibility, but with only indifferent success. Various American libraries began printing cards for their own use between 1890 and 1900. The American Library Association undertook through its Publishing Board to supply printed cards for certain sets and serials. Finally the Library of Congress, which had begun in 1899 to print cards for copyrighted books, undertook in 1901 to apply this method not alone to copyright entries but to all its books, and to sell its cards to other libraries. Thus the Library of Congress became in effect a central cataloguing bureau for the United States—and for other countries—so far as its cards met the needs of other libraries.'

It was Herbert Putnam who launched the massive production and distribution to other libraries of Library of Congress cards; and it is therefore he, and the pioneer Jewett, who can take most credit for the promotion of the concept of cooperative cataloguing: that is, cataloguing for more than just one library. This same concept lay behind the launching in Britain in 1950 of the services of the *British national bibliography*. The culmination of the concept, for both the United States and Great Britain, came a little later, with the Library of Congress's MARC project, linked here with the BNB. MARC is an acronym (MAchine-Readable Cataloguing) for the project, which supplies cataloguing data centrally for current books in the form of magnetic tape which individual libraries can then use, through the medium of a computer, to produce their own catalogue entries. Though the data for each book is offered in a very full form, each individual library is able to select only what it considers relevant for its own catalogue. MARC's coverage is very wide; it cooperates with other national cataloguing agencies, and there is now in

173

existence an international network supplying cataloguing data to the Library of Congress. Only in this way can libraries now control bibliographically the modern world's publishing output.

By way of a conclusion to this brief survey of the history of modern cataloguing, reference must be made to the publication in 1953 of what has been responsibly regarded as a milestone in modern thinking, Seymour Lubetzky's *Cataloging rules and principles: a critique of the ALA rules for entry and a proposed design for their revision.*

Lubetzky states the two main objectives of a library catalogue to be these:

—'The first objective is to enable the user of the catalogue to determine readily whether or not the library has the book he wants.'

—'The second objective is to reveal to the user of the catalogue, under one form of the author's name, what works the library has by a given author and what edition or translations of a given work.'

He then goes on to indicate the 'basic conditions and principles' in the following terms: 'The prevailing type of material which is found in a library and is recorded in its catalogue is the book; and the most important characteristic of the book, for the purposes of cataloguing, is the fact that it is provided with a prominent identification tag in the form of a title page. The cataloguer can thus anticipate how a particular book will normally be cited and looked for and provide for it accordingly. The title page generally includes the name of the author and the title of the book, sometimes only the title of the book, and occasionally only the name of the author. The name of the author and the title of the book are therefore the most important clues by which the book will be identified when cited, and by which it will be looked for in the catalogue or called for in the library. The principles and rules for the entry of books must consequently be based on these two elements, and will apply similarly to other materials identified by an author, or title, or both.'

174

Lubetzky's theory is not to be denied: that the identifying tag for a modern book is its title-page, and the most important clues to a book's identity are the name of its author and its title. However, the false step from this reasoning—a step shown to be false by some three thousand years of library history—is that therefore all a library needs is an author-title catalogue. A library—which by definition is a store of knowledge—must have a subject catalogue. Librarians as such sometimes see a library catalogue primarily as an inventory; as a principle, this is also supported by library history—a list of a library's contents must be provided; but the corresponding principle, relating to the need for a subject catalogue, is no less important.

Norris, at the end of her survey of the history of cataloguing from 1100 to 1850, sums up the argument thus: 'The catalogue has been traced through all its forms, from the systematic-classed ones of the ancient world to the haphazard-classed ones of the early nineteenth century. The early centuries of the Christian era saw the catalogue as a mere list of books arranged, generally, in some subject order. With the closing of the monasteries, and the transference of book collections to colleges and private hands, a new attitude arose; a catalogue was seen to be something more than an inventory of books; it was a key to the library; the art required for its compilation was acknowledged, and also the fact that it could be formed according to different plans, which again must be governed by certain fixed rules. As a result, many methods sprang up, some of them purely artificial; these in time vanished leaving the author alphabetical and the classed catalogues as the most practical forms.'

References

1 Quoted in IRWIN, R: *The origins of the English library*, 1958.

2 THOMPSON, J W: *Ancient libraries*, 1940.

3 JOHNSON, E D: *History of libraries in the western world*, 2nd ed, 1970.

4 NORRIS, D M: *A history of cataloguing*, 1939.

5 PARSONS, E A: *The Alexandrian Library*, 1952.

6 JOHNSON, E D: *op cit*, 3.

7 THOMPSON, J W: *op cit*, 2.

8 PINNER, H L: *The world of books in classical antiquity*, 1958.

9 JOHNSON, E D: *op cit*, 3.

10 CLARK, J W: *The care of books*, 1901.

11 KER, N R, *ed*: *Medieval libraries of Great Britain*, 2nd ed, 1964.

12 NORRIS, D M: *op cit*, 4.

13 SAYERS, W C B: *An introduction to library classification*, 9th ed, 1955.

14 EDWARDS, E: *Memoirs of libraries*, 1859.

15 Quoted in IRWIN, R: *op cit*, 1.

16 SAYERS, W C B: *op cit*, 13.

17 KELLY, T: *A history of public libraries in Great Britain, 1845-1965*, 1973.

18 BLISS, H E: *The organization of knowledge in libraries and the subject approach to books*, 2nd ed, 1939.

19 EDWARDS, E: *op cit*, 14.

20 BLISS, H E: *op cit*, 18.

21 RIDER, F: *Melvil Dewey*, 1944.

22 KELLY, T: *op cit*, 17.

23 SAYERS, W C B: *op cit*, 13.

24 BATTY, C D: *An introduction to Colon Classification*, 1966.

25 MILLS, J: *The Bliss and Colon classifications. Library Association record*, 53 (5) May 1951, 146-153.

26 PALMER, B I: *Itself an education*, 1962.

27 RANGANATHAN, S R: *Philosophy of library classification*, 1951.

28 NORRIS, D M: *op cit*, 4.

29 Quoted in NORRIS, D M: *op cit*, 4.

30 SHARP, H A: *Cataloguing*, 1935.

31 KELLY, T: *op cit*, 17.

32 Quoted in SHARP, H A: *op cit*, 30.

33 SHARP, H A: *op cit*, 30.

34 BISHOP, W W: *Practical handbook of modern library cataloguing*, 2nd ed, 1924.

35 KELLY, T: *op cit*, 17.

CHAPTER EIGHT

The physical design of libraries

1 PALACES AND TEMPLES

The earliest libraries in the world were invariably connected with palaces or temples. The reasons for this, argues John Willis Clark, (1) are because priests under all civilizations have been the learned class, while despots have patronised art and literature, and because such a location was thought to offer greater security.

The Library at Nineveh was housed in the palace of Ashurbanipal (668-626BC). The clay tablets, each a few inches square, were kept in earthen jars, and these jars were kept in rows on shelves in various rooms in the palace. On the wall of each such room, beside the door, was a list of that room's contents. Ashurbanipal's intention, it will be recalled from previous chapters, was to make his Library available to his subjects.

The typical library in classical Greece was usually associated with a school or temple, with special rooms off colonnaded approaches to the temple itself. Inside the library rooms the rolls were kept in pigeon-holes or on shelves on the walls. Elmer D Johnson observes (2) that the Temple of Athena in Pergamon is, following the excavation of its ruins, 'our best example of a Hellenic library'. He describes it as follows: 'The plan of the library may have been adopted from that of Aristotle's in Athens, with the library rooms located off a colonnade, in this case the north colonnade of

178

the Temple. The largest library room, some forty-five by fifty-five feet in area, had a narrow platform about three feet high around three sides. Behind the platform the walls had holes that could have held shelf brackets, or served to anchor book cases. Assuming pigeonholes for rolls located on three walls, this room could have held only about seventeen thousand rolls, indicating that other rooms must have been used for library purposes at the time of its largest size. A bench kept the readers away from the rolls, and may have provided a place where they could be unrolled for examination. In the middle of one end of this room was the statue of the Greek goddess, Athena, to whom this temple was dedicated.'

Contemporaneous with Pergamon of course was the greatest of all Hellenic libraries, the Alexandrian (founded between 300 and 290BC). Edward Alexander Parsons paints the following picture of it: 'Here in ten great Halls, whose ample walls were lined with spacious *armaria*, numbered and titled, were housed the myriad manuscripts containing the wisdom, knowledge, and information, accumulated by the genius of the Hellenic peoples. Each of the ten Halls was assigned to a separate department of learning . . . The Halls were used by the scholars for general research, although there were smaller separate rooms for individuals or groups engaged in special studies.' And Theodore W Koch notes (4) that, according to a remark made by the last great Roman historian, Ammianus Marcellinus (AD 330-395), nothing could compare with the richness of the architecture of the Alexandrian Library except the Capitol in Rome.

James Westfall Thompson observes (5) that in ancient times a library building almost always, like the temples themselves, faced the east. For libraries this was a very practical arrangement: it gave early access to the morning sun, and thus ensured the dissipation of night damp (which was of course injurious to papyrus and parchment). Johnson adds (6) that Vitruvius, a first century Roman writer on architecture, declared that it was always considered correct to place the library rooms of a mansion on the east side, so as to have the best light for reading.

Thompson also supplies a description of the library of Celsus at Ephesus, constructed in Roman imperial times: 'The main room was a large one, in which stood a statue of Athene. In the walls were niches about nine feet high and three feet broad, once lined with wood and closed with doors; these were the presses. The second storey formed a gallery supported by pillars running around the upper part of the main room, which was two stories in height. The walls holding the bookcases were separated from the outer walls of the structure by a space about a yard wide which evidently served the purpose of protecting the "inside shell" from earth damp and the moisture of the atmosphere, and at the same time facilitated admission to the gallery. In the foundation, under the apse in which the figure of Athene stood, was the burial vault of the donor.'

He goes on to describe an even more important library, that built by Hadrian (Emperor from AD 117 to 138) in Athens: 'The foundations consist of blocks of stone. The library is divided into two parts, a huge court of columns in the west and a connecting series of halls and rooms on the east. The ground plan forms a great rectangle of 122 meters by 82 meters. One entered by the hall of columns. The walls of the east room are preserved, in which are niches, once filled with books. The remains answer to the description of the library given by Pausanias (i. 18). The ceilings were resplendent in gold and alabaster. Mural paintings illustrative of the *Iliad* and the *Odessey*, and statues of Homer, Sophocles, and other lights of Greek literature, adorned the great room. In a Greek library the statue or bust of Homer was always present, and from this practice the main hall was sometimes known as the Homereion. In a Roman library the statue or bust of Vergil was invariably found in company with those of illustrious poets, dramatists, historians, orators. Even distinguished living men were sometimes so honored. Cicero describes his gratification because his bust stood opposite that of Aristotle in Atticus' library.'

Thompson also confirms that all such libraries were erected near and were under the protection of a temple,

180

usually to the goddess Athene-Minerva. The colonnades of the temple connected with the library, as in the Porticus Octaviae.

John Willis Clark stresses the point that Roman libraries were cultural places. They were meeting places, reading-rooms, and for conversation. Both Thompson and Johnson illustrate this point further. Thompson recounts that' 'The book room of the Bibliotheca Ulpiana was behind the colonnades surrounding the forum. The place under these colonnades was frequently the reading room, and always a popular spot for conversation or meditation. The great hall in these libraries was often used for public meetings. In his old age Augustus used to hold meetings of the Senate in the Palatine Library. Public readings, lectures, and rhetorical contests were often held in them.' And Johnson adds that the Ulpian Library, founded by the Emperor Trajan in 114 AD, was moved early in the fourth century to the Baths of Diocletian: 'There was a theater and lecture room along with the Baths, so that it was more of a gentlemen's club than a public bath'. Johnson suggests that other Roman libraries might have been associated with baths also.

Clark notes that the libraries of Rome tended to be richly-decorated. This will have already been apparent from the description of the library built by Hadrian in Athens. H L Pinner fills out some of the detail as follows: (7) 'As far as can be judged from ruins, the great public libraries had a Great Hall, which probably served as a reading-room. This was lavishly equipped with coloured marble, alabaster and precious metals, and there was no lack of frescoes and excessive plastic decoration. Cassiodorus even tells of artificial lighting of great brightness. Isidore mentions shelves of cedarwood and ebony. The store-rooms, on the other hand, where there were any at all, were badly kept. The scrolls lay on open shelves. The parchment labels with the titles hung out. Codices and, in Alexandria, even scrolls, were kept in chests.'

Finally, to complete this brief survey of the physical design of libraries in ancient times, mention may be made of the disquisition supplied by Raymond Irwin (8) on the colonnades and cloisters which were such a conspicuous architectural feature of libraries in both classical and mediaeval times. Irwin argues that it is unlikely that the monastic cloister is a direct descendant of the classical colonnade, but that both resulted from their being the natural solution to the problem of providing a sheltered area for reading (usually out loud) and discussion. They did not need glazing; they afforded protection from wind and rain and extremes of weather; and they let in natural light. Thus the basic design of an early library was a series of store-rooms fitted with either pigeon-holes or cupboards in which the rolls were kept, and a range of covered walks where they were consulted by readers. It was not usual for books to be both stored and read in the same room. Irwin comments that this system must have raised problems of security, but can offer no evidence of what methods were used to prevent books being taken away from libraries in classical times.

From the foregoing brief account there is confirmation of a number of the principles of librarianship already adumbrated in previous chapters of the present work. First, there is solid confirmation of the principle that libraries are created by society. Every ancient library was centrally located in its community and firmly attached to its main institutions. The same circumstances also endorse another principle, namely, that libraries are conserved by society. Thirdly, the actual physical set up of libraries such as Ashurbanipal's and that at Alexandria illustrates that a library's purpose is the storage and dissemination of knowledge. Fourthly and lastly, the connection of ancient libraries with either palaces or temples demonstrates that they were regarded as centres of power.

2 MONASTERIES, CATHEDRALS AND COLLEGES
Just as the libraries of ancient times were invariably connected with either palaces or temples, so also were mediaeval libraries associated with the institution which in their era represented the heart of society and the centre of temporal as well as spiritual power: the Church.

In the many early monasteries, life centred around the cloister, even in the uncertain and occasionally harsh climates of Northern European countries. It was in the cloister therefore that the books were kept. As a monk of Ramsey Abbey in Huntingdonshire complained: 'In vento minime pluvia nive sole sedere / Possumus in claustro nec scribere neque studere' (As we sit in wind, rain, snow and sun, we can neither write nor study in the cloister)' (9)

The books were housed in a recess in the wall of the cloister, or in a book-room nearby, or in book-presses in the cloister. A 'library' of this period was therefore long and narrow, open (glazed or unglazed) to the light on one long side, screened off at one or both of the narrow sides, with books on the inner long wall. Such a library would also have carrels for the older monks. These carrels would be like sentry-boxes in shape, one side formed by a light (that is, one of the perpendicular divisions of a mullioned window) of the window looking into the garth (the central grass-plot or courtyard), opposite which would be a door of modest height (so as to allow supervision and to admit as much light as possible into the cloister-library). The function of a carrel was not to give its user some privacy (which was discouraged), but to provide a degree of comfort. In the carrel itself, there would be a seat on one side and a desk on the other, arranged so that the light fell on the reader's left-hand.

Along the cloister wall there would usually run a bench. Clark records that at Durham, the cloister was glazed, but whether the glass was white or stained he was not able to ascertain. At Bury St Edmunds and at Peterborough the glass was stained—the latter cloister depicting, among other subjects, the history of the Old Testament.

The next developments came as a result of the growth during the fourteenth and fifteenth centuries of monastic collections, in most cases from a few hundred books to a few thousand. Places in which to keep books, in addition to the cloister, had to be found. Clark cites the case of the parent-house of the Cistercian order at Citeaux, a large and wealthy monastery in Burgundy. The books were scattered all over the House, wherever a spare corner could be found for them, according to a catalogue compiled by John de Cirey, who was Abbot there at the end of the fifteenth century.

Instead of *armaria*, or book-chests, a special room would be constructed to hold books. This was usually built over some existing building, or over the cloister. Windows were very much featured, and the majority of such rooms were long and narrow. Typical examples, built over the cloister, were Lincoln, Salisbury, St Paul's and Wells; likewise at the Abbey of St Germain de Près, where the library was placed over the south walk of the cloister in 1555, and eventually invaded the west side also, its united length then being some 384 feet.

In some places, separate library buildings were constructed. Clark notes examples at Lichfield Cathedral (60ft x 15ft, approached by a flight of stairs), begun in 1489 and completed in 1493; Noyon, near Amiens (72ft x 17ft, approached by means of an external staircase); and the Cathedral of Rouen (105ft x 25ft, access being obtained directly from the transept by way of a stone staircase in two flights), completed in 1482. Elmer D Johnson also mentions the cathedral library at York, finished in 1421, which had two floors, with books upstairs and a study downstairs.

College libraries, as Clark observes, certainly inherited the general style of monastic libraries, even though, ironically, the collegiate system 'was to a certain extent established to counteract monastic influence'. The internal fittings of collegiate and monastic libraries tended to be identical.

A purpose-built room for a library was not introduced into the plan of the Oxford and Cambridge colleges for more than a century after their foundation. The characteristics of such rooms was their equidistant windows; these windows did not differ from those of ordinary rooms except that they were separated by much smaller intervals. The earliest of these libraries in existence in England was the upper chamber (solarium) which Thomas Cobham, Bishop of Worcester, began to build over the old Congregational House, Oxford, about 1320;

this room was about 45ft long by 18ft broad, with seven single-light windows on each side and a window of two lights at the east end. Another example is the old library of Queen's College, Cambridge; this room is on the first floor of the north side of the quadrangle, forming part of the buildings erected in 1448; it is 44ft long by 20ft wide, and lighted by eleven windows each of two lights, six in the south wall and five in the north. The ground-plan shows the desks between the windows (2ft wide); the books lay on the desks and were chained to it. A bench for the reader was placed between each pair of desks. Clark calls this the 'lectern-system', and records that it was adopted, with various modifications, in England, France, Holland, Germany and Italy.

After the 'lectern-system' came the 'stall-system' (exemplified, for example, in the library of Corpus Christi College, Oxford, built in the early sixteenth century): a double-sided bench with on either side of it a consultation ledge, and above and below the two ledges, shelves of books, the whole forming, with the window between the bookcases, a kind of compartment. The books on the shelves were chained, until eventually chains fell into disuse. The material of the bookcases was oak or deal, and usually very plain (even rough). The floors of such rooms were wooden, or tiled. The consultation ledges were sometimes hinged. The stall-system is almost certainly monastic in origin.

Johnson supplies some additional details of fittings and accommodation. He notes, for example, that candles and lamps were usually forbidden in the library rooms for fear of fire; that sometimes the collections were divided into two parts, one for general public use and the other for more restricted use; and that there were various devices employed to make books more readily available, such as the book-wheel (which was something like a water-wheel with a number of books arranged on it so that a reader standing in one position could consult as many as a dozen different volumes in succession without moving from his original position), and the circular (or hexagonal or octagonal) desk (a similar arrangement to the book-wheel but on a horizontal plane, whereby a reader walked around to consult the books laid out on its top—or, in the few instances where the desk top was attached to an axle, rotated it). Johnson also observes that the custom of chaining books to the desks began not with the most valuable ones, but with the ones most used; later, after the coming of the printed book, many manuscript volumes were chained simply for safe-keeping.

Speaking in general of the physical design of mediaeval libraries, Clark stresses their simplicity in terms of appointments. Nor did they provide much degree of comfort. A print by Jan Cornelis Woudanus of the library of the University of Leyden shows that so great was the number of book-cases in the room, the readers had to consult them standing. And the books were not only chained, but very often chained too close together for convenience.

However, he also points to a number of more attractive features. Elaborate catalogues enabled readers to find what they wanted in the shortest possible time. Globes, maps and astronomical instruments were provided to give them further assistance in their studies. In some places, the library served the purpose of a museum, and curiosities of various kinds were stored in it. In many instances, the bookcases were not plain and rough, but beautifully carved and decorated. The floor-tiles were sometimes worked in patterns, the walls decorated with plaster-work in relief, and the roof-timbers ornamented with the coat-armour of benefactors.

Of such embellishments, the most distinctive were the stained-glass windows. Clark cites the twelve windows at St Albans, which contained figures illustrating the subjects of books placed near them: Rhetoric and Poetry, for example, were represented by Cicero, Sallust, Musaeus and Orpheus.

It may be left to Johnson to sum up briefly the physical design of libraries in the mediaeval period: 'By the fifteenth century, separate library buildings were being erected—usually long, narrow rooms lighted by many tall windows. The shape of the room was designed to make as much use of natural light as possible, but it was also probably influenced by the fact that prior to being placed in separate buildings, libraries had often been housed in rooms over arcades or open corridors. Inside the rooms, the book-desks were located between the windows, so that the light fell directly on the reading shelf. Book-stalls or carrels were being used by the fifteenth century, with tall bookcases of four to six shelves providing separate booths for readers.' (10)

3 THE AGE OF MAGNIFICENCE

In terms of the design of libraries, the sixteenth century onwards may be described as the age of magnificence. Not until the twentieth century were the functions of libraries allowed to dictate the details of their physical form, and even now the tradition of the prestigious and monumental building lingers on. There is little point in outright professional criticism of this tradition since it has always been a first principle that libraries are the creation of society, and it must therefore follow that they will reflect primarily society's view of them. Thus a monarch or a prince of the Church will always erect a palatial library building, a patriotic state will always want a national library that is positively monumental, proud city fathers will always go for bourgeois splendour in their principal local library, and a plebian society will aim to achieve some kind of 'people's palace'. What a librarian might or might not want in the way of practical and technical requirements has necessarily always come second in the design of libraries.

Sometimes, of course, the architect has succeeded in combining his society's view and his society's convenience; and this was true of the outstanding library building of the sixteenth century, the Biblioteca Laurenziana, or Medicean Library, at Florence. After the death of Pope Leo X in 1521, his executor Cardinal Giulio dei Medici restored to the city of Florence the books which their ancestors had collected, and commissioned Michelangelo to build a library to house them. The library was formally opened in 1571. Michelangelo so designed it that it was raised high above the ground, and therefore well-lighted and ventilated. The approach to it was by way of a double staircase of marble. Its dimensions were 151ft 9in long by 134ft 4in broad, and it was provided with 15 windows in each of the side walls placed at about 7ft 6in from the floor. The flat wooden roof was carved, and the terracotta pavement was of yellow design on a red ground. On each side of the room were 44 desks, richly ornamented, with books lying on each desk or on the shelf beneath it. The stained glass in the windows depicted heraldic subjects and the arms of the Medici occupied a central position in each.

Outstanding for quite another reason was the library at the Escorial, Madrid, which Philip II began in 1563 and completed in 1584. In this library the principle of wall-shelving was first introduced. The library itself was 212ft long, 35ft broad and 36ft high. The roof was a barrel-vault, painted in fresco; on the walls was a great frieze of historical scenes and celebrities. The room was lighted by windows, 13ft high, which extended down to the floor, and by other smaller windows just under the vault. In the wall-space between each pair of high windows were fitted bookcases, made of mahogany inlaid with ebony, cedar and other woods, over 12ft high.

Another library of the period in which the wall-system was adopted was the Biblioteca Ambrosiana at Milan, built and furnished by Cardinal Borromeo between 1603 and 1609. This was in the form of a single ground-floor hall, 74ft long by 29ft broad. The walls were lined with bookcases about 13ft high, protected by wire-mesh. At each corner of the hall was a staircase leading to a 2ft 6in wide gallery furnished with 8ft 6in bookcases. Above this was a frieze of saints' portraits. The roof was again a barrel-vault, ornamented with plaster-work. The library was lighted by two huge semi-circular windows, one at each end. The floor was of plain tiles; there were four tables, one in each corner; and there was a central brazier. Clark supplies an impressive photograph, taken in 1899, of what he rightly describes as 'this noble room'.

Another equally impressive library of the seventeenth century was that of Cardinal Mazarin, built (in Clark's phrase) 'in accordance with his magnificent ideas'. It was furnished at the end of 1647, and not only incorporated the wall-system of shelving used at the Escorial but, in Clark's opinion, drew overall inspiration from it.

The earliest example in England of wall-shelving was introduced in the eastern wing of the Bodleian, completed with its fittings in 1612; this was lined with a bookcase extending from floor to ceiling. Clark observes that it was Sir Christopher Wren who, though he did not actually introduce the wall-system into England, developed it, adapted it to national requirements, and 'by the force of his genius shewed what structural changes were necessary in order to meet the increased number of books to be accommodated'.

Wren's first piece of library work was at Lincoln Cathedral in 1674. He placed a continuous bookcase along the north wall of the room, extending from floor to ceiling. A general description of the library is given by Clark in the following terms: 'The building consists of an arcade of nine semicircular arches supported on eight Doric columns. The upper storey, containing the library, has eleven windows in a similar classical style, and above there is a bold entablature ornamented with acanthus leaves. The library is 104ft long by 17ft 6in wide and 14ft high; the ceiling is flat and perfectly plain. In addition to the windows above mentioned there is another at the west end. The entrance is at the east end through a richly ornamented door. The shield in the centre of the pediment bears the arms of Dean Honywood.'

Wren also planned the New Library for Trinity College, Cambridge, the building of which was begun in 1675-76. Clark notes that he seems to have borrowed the general design of the Library of St Mark at Venice, begun by Sansovino in 1536. At Trinity College Wren combined the wall-system of shelving with the medieval at-right-angles system to produce a series of what he called 'celles'. As well as praising Wren's 'masterly combination' of fittings, Clark also refers to the library's 'beauty of external design'.

Wren's next example of library work was the library of St Paul's Cathedral, again combining (in Clark's phrase) 'an ingenuity of contrivance and a dignity of conception'. Clark is also confident of the influence on its design of the Biblioteca Ambrosiana. The library was completed towards the end of the first decade of the eighteenth century.

Clark concludes his account of Wren's library work by observing that his influence can be traced in all the library fittings erected at Cambridge in the eighteenth century. At Emmanuel College, for example, between 1702 and 1707, the tall bookcases set up at right angles to the walls in 1679, were moved forward and shelves in continuation of them placed against the side-walls.

Before leaving English library buildings and fittings of the eighteenth century, it is worth noting briefly that the chaining of books continued 'with strange persistency' (Clark's phrase) far into the modern period. It was only towards the end of the eighteenth century that the practice was finally abandoned. The books at Eton College were not unchained until 1719; at the Bodleian, the removal began in 1757; at King's College, Cambridge, the books were unchained in 1777; at Brasenose College, Oxford, in 1780; and at Merton College, Oxford, not until 1792.

National library buildings as a genre, from the eighteenth century onwards, have epitomised the architectural ideals of the age of magnificence. A glance through the photographs of buildings in the first edition of Arundell Esdaile's survey of national libraries (12) makes this abundantly clear: landscaped settings, vast flights of steps and stairways, monumental facades, great courtyards and domes, lofty columns internally and externally, enormous reading halls, long vistas of wall-shelving and galleries, richly-carved tables and desks, ornate ceilings with decorative light-fittings, elaborate fenestration, beautiful tiled floors, friezes and frescoes and statues on pedestals. However, a few specific examples may also be cited in illustration.

From the eighteenth century, there is the Nationalbibliothek at Vienna. In 1723-6, under Charles VI, a library building in the Baroque style was erected. Esdaile describes it thus: 'The main feature . . . was a magnificent hall, 241 feet in breadth and 62 feet in height, decorated with marble Corinthian pillars, a statue of Charles VI in the middle, and other statues of princes of the Empire round the hall. In the middle of the ceiling was an oval cupola, round the cupola and on the ceilings on each side were frescoes painted by Daniel Gran between 1726-30.'

Later that century, in 1759, the collections which became the British Museum Library were placed in Montague House in London. This had been the town mansion of the Lords Montague of Boughton in Northamptonshire. It was built by the French architect, Pierre Puget, and was (in Esdaile's words) 'a dignified . . . building of beautiful proportions'. Eventually, in 1823, the acquisition of the library of King George III doubled the size of the museum's book collections, and the Trustees were forced to consider finding extra accommodation. As Esdaile records, they decided 'on a grandiose new building, and Sir Robert Smirke designed it for them in the Greek style, to which the Elgin marbles irresistably tempted them, consisting of four wings enclosing a vast quadrangle'.

In 1780, in Berlin, Frederick the Great opened his new library. It was a square building, with two curved wings from each side, terminating in two unequal corner pavilions. Again Esdaile's description emphasises its general magnificence: 'The strong four-square ground floor with its small windows served only as a support for the richly decorated upper half, and was moreover not at the disposal of the Library, being used partly by the garrison as a warehouse and partly by the opera house. Over the middle bow window was the motto 'Nutrimentum spiritus'. The first storey, which was the Library proper, comprised a square middle room and the two bow-shaped wings; in the corners were enclosed the pavilions. The books were shelved against the wall so that no projections might spoil the unbroken view of the room. In the neighbouring house a reading room was instituted. It was essentially a state room in the eighteenth century grand style.'

A final example, from the very end of the nineteenth century, is the Library of Congress building. Until 1897 the library occupied part of the Capitol, but in 1888 Congress had passed an Act for the erection of a separate library building and $4M were appropriated for the purpose. The plans for the new building were drawn up by General Thomas Casey on a massive scale: the floor space of the original structure amounted to nearly eight acres. The style was Italian Renaissance, with much use of granite and marble, and the interior embellished with sculpture and paintings.

Public libraries, which began to be established during the nineteenth century, were launched modestly in building terms, but they also eventually achieved a degree of magnificence. Thomas Kelly in his history of public libraries in Great Britain (13) records that in the period 1845-1886 few libraries were so fortunate as to occupy premises built for them. Most local authorities provided accommodation as cheaply as possible—by finding a room somewhere or by converting an existing building. Oxford's public library in 1854 was housed in a disused town hall; at Leeds, the accommodation was the old infirmary; and at Northampton, after twelve years in the town hall itself, the library was lodged from 1884-1889 in a converted county gaol.

It was generally accepted, however, that the basic essentials for a service were a reference library, a lending library, and a reading room. A lecture-hall was also considered desirable; and a few libraries tried to create something of the social atmosphere of the mechanics' institutes—Wandsworth, for example, provided a recreation room with chess, draughts and backgammon, though this particular venture was soon abandoned because of (in the words of Wandsworth's Annual Report for 1885-6) 'unruly behaviour and gambling'.

Kelly notes that branch libraries of that period were built in every conceivable external style from classical to Tudor. He comments that as a genre they possessed 'that solid and gloomy grandeur characteristic of Victorian public buildings'—high ceilings, dark walls, heavy furniture. Of the next period of public library history which he treats, 1887 to 1918, he observes in relation to buildings that they followed no uniform pattern: some looked like Greek temples, some like Renaissance palaces, some like Dissenting chapels, some like Tudor mansions. There was also the problem of 'over-building': that is, the upkeep of a large building often absorbed most of the proceeds from the penny rate, leaving little for actual books. Kelly quotes examples of some extravagant features in a number of buildings: a games room in one, a roof garden as part of another, and even one library with an observatory.

The same taste for magnificence was to be found in American public libraries. Edward Edwards, writing in 1859, (14) describes the Astor Library in New York (opened 1854) as being built after the model of a palace at Florence, and the architecture of the Library of the City of Boston (1858) as being in the Roman Italian style. The 1890s successor to the latter building kept the same magnificent style, and is described by William Warner Bishop (15) as copying 'French and Florentine palace architecture'.

As a concluding note, it may be added that in the modern period academic library buildings have been as much in the tradition of magnificence as their national and public counterparts. Ralph Ellsworth records, (16) for example, that from the middle of the nineteenth century until the 1930s, there was a steady evolution of the research library building with various book storage arrangements and large monumental reading rooms. All such buildings were designed to fit one of the traditional architectural styles—Gothic, Greek, Romanesque or Georgian—so that library functions had to be fitted into space requirements that were determined primarily by architectural considerations, not by the needs of the functions themselves.

4 FORM FOLLOWS FUNCTION
Though the practical and technical requirements of libraries have taken second place to the pursuit of magnificence in

their design for almost the entire period from the sixteenth century onwards, this does not of course mean that such requirements have been ignored. In the previous section of this chapter, for example, it was noted that Michelangelo's design for the Biblioteca Laurenziana took account of the need for good lighting and ventilation; and it may be added, as Clark shows, that Michelangelo's design sketch for the bookcases, which includes a drawing of a human figure on the seat, 'proves the care which he took to ensure a height convenient for readers'.

Then again, in 1627, Gabriel Naudé (17) demonstrated in his pioneer work, *Avis pour dresser une bibliothèque*, a proper concern with a library's environment, not only in the matter of good natural lighting (since in Naudé's time both artificial lighting and heating would have been considered dangerous), but also about the question of humidity (suggesting that a library building should be raised a few steps above the ground to avoid dampness), and how to overcome the problems of 'intemperature of the air' (namely, by building garrets and chambers above the library). Naudé also stipulated that a library should be in the place 'most retired from . . . noise and disturbance', with 'pure air' away from marshes, sinks and dung-hills.

Lighting, heating and ventilation have always presented problems for the designers of library buildings, and most of these problems were not adequately resolved until the coming of the age of technology in the nineteenth and twentieth centuries. Irwin observes (18) that the architectural problems of lighting a large enclosed hall were not really solved until Renaissance times. He reminds us that in classical and mediaeval days, most study was carried out al fresco, in colonnade or cloister: a fine arrangement in a Mediterranean summer, but a severe handicap in a Northern winter. Windows were a rarity in the ancient world, and in any case they were intended principally to let in air rather than light. Glazing was adopted in Roman times, but 'the large sheets of glass and the wide window openings needed for

194

good natural lighting did not begin to make their appearance till the end of the sixteenth century'.

Irwin goes on to point out that the problems of artificial lighting were not solved until relatively recently. First came the use of candles, but these were costly, and dangerous. 'Bodley . . . set his ban on all forms of fire and flame, and this practice was followed generally. Artificial heating caused as much apprehension as artificial light, and the installation of a heating system at the Bodleian in 1845 caused dire consternation until the pipes were safely insulated.' Thus until quite recent times, libraries were open only in daylight hours, and for much of the year 'students were compelled to work in unheated gloom'. This also meant that potential readers were limited to the scholarly or leisured classes, for of course the majority of folk had to work during the daylight hours.

Good oil lamps were not available until the last years of the nineteenth century; and gas lamps with incandescent mantles not until later still—and even then, for a long time, the supply of gas was confined to towns. Eventually of course, came electricity, and with it a revolution in lighting, heating and ventilation arrangements. Even so, it must be remembered that in the modern world electricity supply has been known to fail, not to mention the fact that it has become costly. It is therefore difficult to contradict the view of A E Richardson that 'it is unlikely that artificial light will ever entirely supersede daylight'. (19)

Another library pioneer, Edward Edwards, also promulgated some firm views on the functional requirements of libraries. Writing in 1859, (20) he pointed out that the Laurentian Library at Florence and the Library of St Mark in Venice are noble monuments which enhance the architectural beauty of their respective cities, but, as libraries, are less concerned 'about the practical accommodation of books or of readers'. Of the Library of St Mark he says specifically: 'The building stands out in its impressive beauty, and the books sink into mere accessories'. He also refers to the magnificent Vatican

Library, with its long ranges of sumptuous but 'carefully closed' bookcases, commenting that 'the great majority of the books are as entirely out of sight, as if they were entombed, rather than preserved for purposes of study'. He mentions approvingly, however, the old Library of St Geneviève in Paris, where 'the decorations were, as they always should be, merely accessory'. Of all these early buildings, he says that 'there has been little regard to economy of space, or to the readiest and cheapest provision for future enlargement'. On another score, he condemns the Radcliffe Library at Oxford as being not only 'showy', but also as a building which nobody would ever imagine to be a library.

This preamble from Edwards serves as a reminder that library buildings must reflect all the principles of librarianship, not just some of them. The age of magnificence, described in the previous section, took into account and reflected the principles that libraries are created and conserved by society, and that they are centres of power. The same age fulfilled the principle that libraries are for the storage of knowledge, but did not fully reflect their requirement to disseminate that knowledge to all. Nor, in their design, did libraries of that age make sufficient provision for the principle that libraries must grow.

What really put paid to the library buildings of the age of magnificence was the mass production of printed books. Ellsworth notes (21) that the introduction of the rotary press made library collections become sizeable in the last half of the nineteenth century; until then, wall-shelving was adequate, especially since it could extend several galleries high, as in the 1860s in the Peabody Library in Baltimore. William Warner Bishop (22) sums up the history of European library buildings down to the twentieth century as a process of adapting 'old and generally palatial structures to the use of a steadily increasing number of readers and an overwhelming mass of books'. Having referred to the numerous historical examples of the use of 'a great, ornamental single hall devoted to housing and serving a library' (the library at the

Escorial, for instance), Bishop goes on, like Ellsworth, to pick out the rotary press (invented by Richard Hoe, an American) as the development (coming into general use for the manufacture of books shortly after 1850) which finally 'sounded the doom of the one-hall library'. And Theodore W Koch (23) likewise ascribes the abandonment of the system of putting 'books on parade in a big hall' to the storage problems arising from increasing book numbers.

The British Museum Reading Room, planned by Panizzi, is frequently cited as an example of the adaptation of an existing building to cope with increased numbers of books. This adaptation has been described as 'a complete innovation in functional planning', (24) an 'engineering age' conception in cast iron which made it possible to accommodate a book-stack for some 1,500,000 volumes and places for 450 readers.

Edwards himself supplies further details of this remarkable adaptation. The Reading Room is 140ft in diameter and 106ft high. It is lighted by 20 windows and a glazed aperture in its dome; all the glazing is double and of great strength. Provision was made for the renewal of air by grated openings in the floor connected with the external air by horizontal trunks beneath the surface of the floor, and by louvred openings in the roof. Heating was installed in the form of hot-water pipes. As regards protection against fire, slate and iron were much used in the Reading Room's construction, and only the oak floor and a few doors were inflammable.

It is clear from Edwards's treatise that he was very much against library buildings which were constructed without sufficient regard to books or readers. But conversely, he was equally opposed to such designs as that proposed by Leopoldo della Santa in Florence in 1816, the aim of which was to accommodate in a rectangular building the largest number of books within the smallest proportionate area and at the least possible cost. Edwards remarks drily that Santa's is an excellent model, 'if an immense book-warehouse be the thing wanted'.

Edwards ends his review of library buildings with an attempt 'to reduce into a few general hints the principal conclusions which seem to be derivable'. First, he stresses 'the prime necessity of a clear conception on the part of the promoters of the undertaking of the kind of Library they design to found, and of the objects which they intend it shall subserve'. Then, taking a town library as his particular specification, he recommends that its site be central and such as to permit extension, with light on all sides if possible (that is, in an open space). He wants the building to be fireproof, well-ventilated, and not above two storeys in height. Its proportions should be such that the greater part of the contents of the library should be seen at one view. The books should be accessible without steps or ladders; the reading rooms should be separate from the book-rooms; and there should be sufficient and appropriate offices and work-rooms. The building should be heated, either by open fire-places or by hot-water pipes; and it should have artificial lighting.

Edwards concludes with a typically pungent remark to the effect that 'even eminent architects frequently sacrifice the main purpose of a building to their ideas—real or mistaken—of its external beauty'.

Thomas Kelly provides (25) an overall description of public library buildings in Edwards's time. He reminds us that access to the shelves was not permitted; reading rooms, as was clearly indicated in Edwards's recommendations, were kept separate from the rooms in which the books were kept. High wall-shelving was customary, and it was left to W F Poole, the chief of the Chicago Public Library, to point (at the first Conference of Librarians held in London in 1877) to the disadvantages of this system as opposed to the alternative system then being developed in the United States of low-ceilinged stackrooms with rows of bookshelves a few feet apart, occupying the entire floor space without the use of ladders (this latter recommendation at least having been made by Edwards in 1859). Poole's criticism was that library buildings seemed to have been constructed 'chiefly for show and architectural decoration'. Kelly adds that the kind of change which Poole was trying to promote came however only very slowly.

Kelly also notes that open fires, for which Edwards had such a lingering preference, persisted in some libraries until almost the end of the nineteenth century, though by that time the majority as a rule were centrally heated by means of hot water or steam. Gas-lighting was commonly used, but before the invention of the incandescent mantle the quality of illumination was poor. Gas also was of course a fire risk, not to mention its production of unpleasant and injurious fumes and heat. The introduction of electric lighting caused an 'astonishing transformation' in libraries. It was brought into use in the British Museum Library in 1879, and in the Picton Reading Room at Liverpool in 1881.

Kelly's account of public library buildings in the early years of the twentieth century makes a special mention of the Carnegie Corporation leaflet of 1911, entitled *Notes on the erection of library buildings*. This document recommended a simple rectangular plan, with all library rooms on a single floor, divided as necessary by movable bookshelves and therefore permitting maximum flexibility.

He records that the open access revolution brought about many consequences in its train. Shelving had to be lowered, so island stacks were substituted for lofty wall shelving. Bookstacks had also to be arranged in such as way as to make supervision possible.

W C Berwick Sayers, in his manual of book classification, (26) points to the physical requirements of introducing a classified arrangement in a library—such an arrangement of course being a necessary corollary of any open access system. A classified library needs more room than an unclassified library, because any vacant place will not do for placing a new addition. Also, the ideal library for a classified collection is one large room; a series of rooms is not suitable, and in any case in an open access library is too wasteful of staff. Finally, Sayers reminds us that a primary classification of books is by the characteristic of size; no library can afford the loss of vertical space which would be caused by placing both very small and very large books on the same shelf. Thus division into sizes is required—at least into octavos and smaller books, and into quartos, folios and larger volumes. Hence library shelves should be adjustable, to contend with the balance of growth between sizes.

From Kelly's account it is clear that it was not until the late 1930s that public library buildings began to move towards a simpler, more functional and more contemporary design, away from 'a worship of cliché and historical style' (in the words of E J Carter, Librarian to the Royal Institute of British Architects, writing in 1930–by 1937, he felt that the situation had at least begun to change). The interiors of libraries tended to be more open and flexible, with few separate rooms and permanent dividing walls. Libraries became brighter places, with light colours for paintwork and new flooring materials such as rubber and linoleum. There was also increased window space, made possible by new methods of building construction.

Ellsworth (27) also fixes on the 1930s as the period when academic library design began to be based on library functions, rather than on no more than architectural considerations. He declares that the dedication of Yale's Sterling Library in 1931 marked in America the end of an era, and that from the 1930s onwards there was a shift from 'a purely aesthetic approach to planning to one based primarily on the use and users of buildings'. This change was in line with the new spirit of architecture in the 1920s and 1930s, represented by the phrase, 'Form follows function'.

Prior to the 1930s, Ellsworth argues, (28) the needs of the rapidly changing universities were not yet stabilised and defined; donors still insisted on classical forms; and the technology of building had not yet freed the architect from the limitations of natural lighting and ventilation. In the 1930s all these factors, along with the new school of architectural thought, 'matured sufficiently to permit the planning of a satisfactory research library building'. He adds: 'In one sense we have moved abruptly from the renaissance castle to the modern skyscraper'.

If the new school of architectural thought was the first strong influence on the design of post-1930s academic

200

libraries, then the second has certainly been the modular method of planning libraries conceived by Angus Snead Macdonald. Macdonald's first statement of the method, prepared with the help of Alfred M Githens and entitled *A library of the future* (*Library journal*, LVIII, December 1933), was (in Ellsworth's words) (29) 'a turning point in library architecture'. The first fully modular library buildings began to be erected in the 1940s, the earliest examples being those at Hardin-Simmons University (Texas) and North Dakota State College.

The outcome of these two strong influences was that libraries became simple, flexible (not only because of the modular construction, but also because of movable shelving, low ceiling-heights, and uniform lighting and air-conditioning), box-like structures, with little superficial ornament. However, a third strong influence served to temper this tendency in library building towards being commonplace, architecturally invisible, or even plain ugly. This influence was the wish of the present generation of librarians, in Ellsworth's words, 'to make libraries physically inviting, informal, and easy to use', to provide a building which was 'a machine planned to facilitate certain human activities under conditions of maximum beauty and convenience'.

Much the same sort of development also took place in public library building. Kelly, (30) referring to the boom in public library building in the United Kingdom in the 1950s and 1960s, talks of a 'new look', a contemporary style replacing the previous conventional neo-Georgian or neo-classical exteriors, libraries becoming 'uncompromisingly modern, relying for such beauty as they possessed on a functional arrangement of masses and materials'. The use of steel and concrete gave greater freedom in construction, especially in respect of the provision of large 'picture windows'. Modular construction in public libraries also permitted greater internal flexibility. The basic nucleus was the adult lending library, the adult reference library, and the children's library, with the addition of appropriate specialist rooms— a music and gramophone records room, a local history room.

It also became commoner to talk of 'areas' in an open-plan layout, rather than 'rooms' or 'departments'.

References

1 CLARK, J W: *The care of books*, 1901.

2 JOHNSON, E D: *History of libraries in the western world*, 2nd ed, 1970.

3 PARSONS, E A: *The Alexandrian Library*, 1952.

4 KOCH, T W: *New light on old libraries. Library quarterly*, IV 1934, 244-252.

5 THOMPSON, J W: *Ancient libraries*, 1940.

6 JOHNSON, E D: *op cit*, 2.

7 PINNER, H L: *The world of books in classical antiquity*, 1958.

8 IRWIN, R: *The origins of the English library*, 1958.

9 Quoted in CLARK, J W: *op cit*, 1.

10 JOHNSON, E D: *op cit*, 2.

11 CLARK, J W: *op cit*, 1.

12 ESDAILE, A: *National libraries of the world*, 1934.

13 KELLY, T: *A history of public libraries in Great Britain, 1845-1965*, 1973.

14 EDWARDS, E: *Memoirs of libraries*, 1859.

15 BISHOP, W W: *The historic development of library buildings. In* Fussler, H H *ed: Library buildings for library service*, 1947.

16 ELLSWORTH, R E: *Library buildings. In* Shaw, R R: *The state of the library art*, Vol 3, pt 1, 1960.

17 Quoted in IRWIN, R: *op cit*, 8.

18 IRWIN, R: *op cit*, 8.

19 RICHARDSON, A E: *Library architecture. Library Association record*, 1 (NS) 1923, 87-97.

20 EDWARDS, E: *op cit*, 14.

21 ELLSWORTH, R E: *op cit*, 16.

22 BISHOP, W W: *op cit*, 15.

23 KOCH, T W: *op cit*, 4.

24 *New Encyclopaedica Britannica*, 15th ed, 1974.

25 KELLY, T: *op cit*, 13.

25 SAYERS, W C B: *A manual of classification,* 3rd ed, 1955.

27 ELLSWORTH, R E: *Library architecture and buildings. Library quarterly,* 25 1955, 66-75.

28 ELLSWORTH, R E: *op cit,* 16.

29 ELLSWORTH, R E: *op cit,* 27.

30 KELLY, T: *op cit,* 13.

CHAPTER NINE

The principles revealed

The first principle of librarianship is: *Libraries are created by society.*

An historical survey of libraries, from their origins to the present time, demonstrates beyond contention that their destiny is always bound up with the destiny of their society. The library at Nineveh was inextricably associated with the rule of Ashurbanipal. Under Ashurbanipal and his three predecessors (Sargon, Sennacherib and Esarhaddon), Assyria dominated Western Asia, a kingdom which stretched from the Persian Gulf to the Mediterranean. Ashurbanipal made Nineveh his royal capital, his administrative centre and the heart of his civilisation. And in Nineveh he set up a library, not only as a storehouse of the lore and knowledge of his society, but also as the means for their dissemination.

Similarly, the great Alexandrian Library was established solely to promote the over-riding aspiration of Alexandria itself: that is, to be a focus of all Hellenic learning and culture. The city was founded early in 331BC by Alexander the Great, seeking characteristically to diffuse the language and civilisation of Greece wherever victory led him. His intentions were brought to fruition by one of his generals, Ptolemy Soter, who eventually came to rule Egypt (323-285 BC), and who founded the famous library between 300 and 290BC. Soter created an empire that lasted three centuries, built a city that was a wonder of the earth for seven hundred years, and made a library that was an intellectual beacon for nine hundred years.

The libraries of ancient Rome epitomised Roman civilisation. The libraries of the Middle Ages were the creations of the all-pervading and all-powerful Church. In our own times, from the nineteenth century onwards, the provision of public libraries was a direct outcome of the rise of democracy and the spread of popular education. The rise of democracy meant that libraries could no longer be reserved for an élite, and the spread of education required the intellectual sustenance that libraries provide.

This whole history of the inter-relation of libraries and society is illustrated physically in the development of library buildings. In the beginning, libraries were housed in palaces and temples; and then in monasteries and cathedrals. Next they reflected national pride and aspirations, becoming monumental and grandiose. Now, with the rise of democracy, a library building has become in design a kind of people's palace.

The second principle of librarianship, a corollary of the first, is: *Libraries are conserved by society.*

Despite the depradations caused by the perishability of materials, the carelessness of users, general negligence, theft, malicious damage, atmospheric conditions, bookworms and vermin, and notwithstanding the curatorial efforts of librarians, it is a fact of library history that most harm to books and libraries has been caused by external disasters— sometimes accidental, but very much more commonly the result of social strife, whether political, civil or religious.

In 221BC, Shih Huang Ti, the founder of the Ch'in dynasty, ordered the destruction of all books except those on agriculture, divination and medicine. In Christian times, following the preaching of St Paul, the Ephesians brought out their books on 'curious arts' and burned them.

The Alexandrian Library was consumed by fire during Caesar's Alexandrian War in 48BC, and burned again by the Saracens in 640AD at the instigation of the fanatical Caliph

Omar, who declared that if the writings of the Greeks agreed with the Koran, or book of Allah, then they were unnecessary, and if they did not agree, they were pernicious and had to be destroyed.

Invaders destroyed or dispersed almost every library in Rome and Italy in the fifth century. The imperial library at Constantinople, founded by Constantine the Great in 330, was destroyed by fire in 477. When Carthage was razed, so was its library.

During the Anglo-Saxon period in Britain, monastic libraries were constantly sacked and destroyed. The dissolution of the monasteries by Henry VIII in 1537-9, the Peasants' War in Germany in 1525, the Huguenot wars in France between 1561 and 1589, all took a heavy toll of libraries. Religious strife has an infamous record in the history of libraries: Caliph Omar and Henry VIII are only two in a long procession of names concerned with the destruction of books. In early times, heathens burned Christian literature; in their turn Christians burned heathen books.

In our own times, during the years after 1933 while Germany was under the dictatorship of Hitler, libraries were subjected to book purges and book burnings. As for times of war—in Britain alone, during the second world war, the total book loss as the result of enemy action was over twenty million volumes.

Conversely, when society has been determined to keep its libraries safe, this has been equally apparent historically. In terms of physical accommodation, ancient libraries, for example, were invariably given a location within the secure precincts of a palace or a temple. And then there is the remarkable fact that popular revolutions have often shown a considerable concern for the safety of libraries. At the time of the French Revolution, all religious libraries were declared national property and all the books and manuscripts therein confiscated, as were all the books belonging to the nobility; the resulting eight or so million books were gathered together in general book deposits in various parts of France and arrangements made for their proper care. Similarly, following the Russian Revolution, in the period from 1918 to 1923, a vast number of books and indeed entire libraries, were transferred to the Lenin State Library.

It is clear historically that the most powerful enemies of libraries are beyond the control of the curatorial function of librarians. Librarians, in the matter of conservation, can be no more than good housekeepers; they can reproduce or refurbish library materials—whether clay tablet, papyrus roll, parchment manuscript or printed volume; they can organise and design proper accommodation and environment; and they can superintend use. But they have no power over the ultimate existence of libraries as such. Just as society creates libraries, so does it conserve them.

The third principle of librarianship is: *Libraries are for the storage and dissemination of knowledge.*

When Ashurbanipal founded his library at Nineveh, he was consciously creating a storehouse of religious, historical, geographical, legal and scientific knowledge from all parts of the known world; and furthermore, he plainly intended this storehouse to be of use to his subjects. The Alexandrian Library was, similarly, a universal storehouse of knowledge, containing as it eventually did, almost all of the extant literature. This indeed was the declared and recorded aim of its first librarian, Demetrios of Phaleron. And again, as at Nineveh, the Alexandrian storehouse was created not only to preserve knowledge, but to disseminate it: hence the assembly by the Ptolemies of a great body of scholars to work on the materials gathered there.

The same principle was maintained throughout the Middle Ages, though the emphasis then tended to be on preservation rather than dissemination. It was felt that no monastery or convent could be without books: a conviction expressed in the mediaeval epigram 'claustrum sine armario, castrum sine armamentario' (a monastery without a library is like a castle without an armoury).

The principle of both storage and dissemination has continued into modern times. The British Museum Library in the mid-eighteenth century opened its great store of knowledge to the world, and since then the world has been further enriched by the fruits of the talents and labours of those who were thus able to make use of that knowledge—tens of thousands of individuals, including Wordsworth, Sir Walter Scott, Charles Lamb, Coleridge, Macaulay, Thackeray, Dickens, Karl Marx and George Bernard Shaw among the more famous. The Library of Congress contains practically all of man's recorded knowledge, and offers access to that knowledge to all comers.

For more than twenty-five hundred years libraries have had a virtual monopoly on the storage of knowledge. A library is the only human institution to which an individual can turn for a permanent and comprehensive store of information.

A positive proof of the second part of the principle, namely that libraries are for the dissemination of knowledge as much as for its storage, is the evidence over the centuries that society has always credited libraries with having active moral, social, political and educational effects (hence the destruction of libraries in all periods of history at the instigation of powerful individuals or movements). If libraries had been regarded only as storehouses, none of these effects would have been postulated, because the knowledge which leads to them would have been inert, 'a Talent digged in the ground' (in John Durie's famous phrase).

The fourth principle of librarianship is: *Libraries are centres of power.*

'Nam et ipsa scientia potestas est', wrote Francis Bacon in the seventeenth century. Knowledge is power. And since libraries are storehouses of knowledge, it must follow that they are centres of power. These two facts are reflected in library history in myriad ways.

In the earliest times, libraries were physically associated with temples and palaces, located within the very precincts of spiritual and temporal power. The earliest librarians were drawn from the upper classes, and were of high political or priestly rank. In the Middle Ages, libraries were an integral and crucial part of the Church's trappings of power.

That libraries are centres of power has nowhere been better shown in the modern period than by century upon century of magnificent buildings, from Renaissance examples such as the Medicean Library and the El Escorial library, down to the great national libraries such as that erected in Vienna in the 1720s by Charles VI or that opened in Berlin in 1780 by Frederick the Great.

The connection of libraries with power remains as obvious in our own time. The Library of Congress until 1897 was housed in the Capitol itself, the seat of government of the most powerful nation on earth. But its location there was no more than a direct continuation of a three-thousand year-old tradition: wherever power has rested, whether with monarch or prince of the Church or democratic assembly, that is where the library has been located.

The fifth principle of librarianship is: *Libraries are for all.*

Evidence of public access to libraries exists from the earliest period of their history. In the seventh century BC, Ashurbanipal's large collection of clay tablets was expressly prepared for the instruction of his subjects and placed in the midst of his palace for public use. Edward Edwards described it as a 'public library in clay'. And while Demetrios of Phaleron, the first librarian of the Alexandrian Library, was primarily a collection-builder, his successor, Zenodotus of Ephesus, directed his efforts to making the famous library freely available for public access.

The Athenian tyrant, Peisistratus (c600-528BC) threw open his collection for public use. Throughout Greece, by the end of the third century BC, libraries were to be found in every major city, and research in them could be carried on by any citizen. In Rome, the idea of a public library with large collections of volumes designed for common use first found practical realisation in the time of the first Roman emperor, Augustus (63BC-14AD), who built two public libraries, one in connection with the temple of Apollo on the Palatine Hill, and the Octavian Library on the Campus Martius. And the foundation of the public library by Gaius Asinius Pollo (76BC-4AD), in the Atrium Libertatis on the Aventine Hill, was made memorable by the phrase Pliny used of it, *ingenia hominum rem publicam*—making men's talents and mental powers a public possession.

John Willis Clark, the great historian of medieval libraries, claimed that all such libraries were practically public, and that the monastic libraries were the public libraries of the Middle Ages. Elmer D Johnson, another notable historian of libraries, has written however that it was the libraries of the mediaeval universities which effectively gave impetus to the idea that libraries should not only preserve the heritage of the past but also open it up to general use. Yet a third historian, C Seymour Thompson, has maintained that a truly public library was not possible before the Renaissance and the Reformation.

This new spirit manifested itself in the seventeenth century in the writings of Gabriel Naudé and John Durie. Naudé declared of his library that: 'It shall be open to all the world, without excluding a living soul'. Durie wrote that a library is 'no more than a dead Bodie' unless 'animated with a publick Spirit to keep and use it'.

But it was not until the public library movement of the nineteenth century, in Britain and in the United States, that the principle that libraries are for all came to full fruition. This principle now operates throughout the world, and is reflected in (and indeed dictates) library systems and design.

The sixth principle of librarianship is: *Libraries must grow.*

Even in the Middle Ages, when in the earliest period a library was usually no more than a collection of a few hundred codices kept in a bookchest or two in the corner of a monastery chapel, libraries grew. They grew, first, because even the modest libraries of those times had to achieve a certain size before they could be considered adequate by their users—for example, there was the Benedictine rule which required that at least one book should be provided for each of the brethren; and they grew, secondly, because mediaeval libraries, in common with all other libraries of all other times, had to respond to and reflect the growth of learning—their religious beginnings had to be augmented by the fruits of the humanistic revival. The mediaeval university libraries in particular, studying law and medicine, grammar and logic, could not be served by libraries which did not increase steadily in size and range. Library collections can never be stable, or stand still.

In truth, in mediaeval times, library growth was slow and difficult. The number of books could only be increased by the efforts of the copyists: the monks in the *scriptorium* whom the precentor drilled and kept at work, copying texts as part of their regular duties. But by the end of the Middle Ages, in the fourteenth and fifteenth centuries, the number of books in the majority of monastery and cathedral libraries had increased from a few hundred to a few thousand. Thus the lamp of learning was kept burning, however dimly, in the period between the devastation of the great libraries of antiquity and the revival that came with the Renaissance and the spread of printing.

The age of printing, and especially the invention in the nineteenth century of the rotary press, brought about the mass production of books. Libraries therefore not only grew, as they had always done, but did so at an overwhelming rate. The palatial structures of European libraries had to be radically adapted to keep pace with the increase in the number of books. The day of the one-hall library, with books on parade on wall-shelving, was soon over.

National libraries, public libraries and academic libraries all afford striking examples of the principle that libraries must grow. The Library of Congress, for instance, was formally founded in 1800; by 1807, it had a collection of some 3,000 volumes; it was destroyed by British soldiers in 1814, but re-established in the following year with the purchase of ex-President Thomas Jefferson's library of 6,487 volumes; by 1836 it had grown to 24,000 volumes; there was a further partial destruction, by fire, in 1851, but even so, by 1863, the number of volumes was 79,214. Just over a hundred years after, in the early 1970s, it contained no less than 16,000,000 volumes and 30,000,000 manuscripts, which along with various other categories of material (such as

211

gramophone records, reels of film, photographs, maps and so on), made all told some 64,000,000 items. As for the growth of public libraries, a striking example here is the New York Public Library: though not founded until 1895, it contained by the early 1970s a total of some 8,500,000 volumes. Academic libraries have grown just as dramatically; indeed, Fremont Rider calculated that American university libraries doubled in size every sixteen years. Harvard, founded in 1683, had 12,000 volumes by the 1780s; in 1831, 39,605 volumes; in 1849, 96,200 volumes; in 1876, 227,650 volumes; in 1900, 560,000 volumes; in 1925, 2,416,500 volumes; in 1938, 3,941,359 volumes; and by the 1970s, was well on the way to 9,000,000 volumes.

On the basis of the foregoing figures there is plainly no denying the principle that libraries must grow. What the world of librarianship seems now to be awaiting is the emergence of some corollary principle or principles which meet the problems of seemingly infinite and massive growth in every type of major library. However, incredible though it may appear to have to state, library history possibly indicates that such an expectation may be premature. Libraries, though indeed they must grow, do not survive for ever: the great Alexandrian Library, after all, disappeared; and just about all the books in the eight hundred or so mediaeval religious libraries in Britain were destroyed. Also, the clay tablet, the papyrus roll and the parchment codex were all, in turn and in time, overtaken: there is no historical reason why the printed book should not likewise be superseded.

The seventh principle of librarianship is: *A national library should contain all national literature, with some representation of other national literatures.*

In his library at Nineveh, Ashurbanipal collected every Assyrian work he could obtain: religious texts, prayers, incantations, rituals, charms; materials on history, government, geography, law, legends, mythology, astronomy, astrology, biology, mathematics, medicine, natural history; and government publications, such as letters to and from ambassadors, and tax-lists. But as well as Assyrian works, there were copies and translations from other nations, including predecessors (represented by translations of Sumerian and Babylonian texts).

The policy of the Alexandrian Library's first librarian, Demetrios of Phaleron, was to collect all the works of the entire inhabited world. The Alexandrian Library aimed to be not only a complete library of Hellenic literature, but also to represent in translation works from other languages: the Hebrew Bible, ancient Egyptian texts, Persian texts, and some Latin literature.

In modern times, the same principle of librarianship has obtained. The British Museum Library's policy with regard to national literature was stated explicitly in the nineteenth century by its greatest librarian, Antonio Panizzi. 'This emphatically *British* library', he wrote, 'ought to be directed most particularly to British works and to works relating to the British Empire, its religious, political and literary as well as scientific history, its laws, institutions, commerce, arts, etc. The rarer and more expensive a work of this description is the more . . . efforts ought to be made to secure it for the library.' The second part of the principle, relating to the need to represent other national literatures also, was referred to in another statement on the same library, now re-named the British Library Reference Division. In the first Annual Report of the British Library (1973-74) the purpose of the newly-christened Reference Division is stated as being 'to collect, by purchase, gift and exchange, not only all British books and such British manuscripts and papers as are appropriate, but as much as possible of the world's important printed material in all subject fields, and manuscripts of foreign origin in certain specialist fields.'

The eighth principle of librarianship is: *Every book is of use.*

In support of this principle there are two kinds of evidence. The first kind relates to the fact that no responsible librarian or scholar, in the wake of the many disasters to libraries that have occurred over the past three thousand years, has been recorded as having felt that even a single one of the books so lost would not have been missed. Assyriologists have celebrated and cherished every clay tablet which has survived from Nineveh. Scholars would delight in the discovery of any text from the Alexandrian Library. Any mediaeval book which has survived the destruction and dispersal of the English monastery libraries is prized. Any text which missed destruction by Shih Huang Ti, the Ephesians, or Caliph Omar, would now be valued. Even the loss of material from the relatively recent past is regretted: Raymond Irwin pointed out, for example, that half the English novels issued between 1770 and 1800, which were the mainstay of the circulating libraries of that time, are no longer to be found.

The second kind of evidence is the recorded witness of librarians and bookmen over the past few centuries. There is Gabriel Naudé's 'perfect Maxime' that 'there is no Book whatsoever, be it never so bad or decried, but may in time be sought for by some person or other'. There is the statement of Edward Edwards on the function of a national library: that it should be an 'encyclopaedical' storehouse, preserving not only 'the monuments of literature, but ephemera also'. There is William Blade's passionate declaration that 'the possession of any old book is a sacred trust', because: 'An old book, whatever its subject or internal merits, is truly a portion of the national history; we may imitate it and print it in fac-simile, but we can never exactly reproduce it; and as an historical document it should be carefully preserved'.

More recent writers have also promoted the principle. Ernest A Savage praised early librarians for having tried to obtain and preserve books of all kinds, 'even those for which they could see no immediate use'. Henry Evelyn Bliss wrote poetically that the bookstacks of libraries are crowded with dead books and books soon to die, but argued nevertheless that all such material needed to be stored somewhere, because: 'Some of it may be precious some day. Some of it, never precious, will have occasional readers.' Fremont Rider, grappling with the problems of the growth in size of research libraries, while not accepting that 'everything needs to be preserved everywhere', nevertheless proposed to make (in miniature form) everything everywhere accessible.

The ninth principle of librarianship is: *A librarian must be a person of education.*

The librarians of ancient Egypt were highly-educated individuals, as indeed were those of ancient Babylonia and Assyria. Demetrios of Phaleron, the first librarian of the Alexandrian Library, was a philosopher and a cultured Athenian man of letters. Of his many successors, all of them famous savants, perhaps the most outstanding was Callimachus of Cyrene, a universal scholar, the father of bibliography, and the greatest bookman of his age.

In ancient Rome, the numerous public libraries were administered in the name of the emperor by a *procurator bibliothecarum*, a post generally conferred upon some recognised scholar. In the time of Hadrian, for instance, the directorship of the Greek and Latin libraries in Rome was held by the sophist L Julius Vestimus.

From the earliest examples, right down through library history, it is the case that every librarian of note has been a person of education. Three great librarians have been singled out in particular in the present work—Edward Edwards, Antonio Panizzi and Melvil Dewey—and each of their biographies demonstrates the validity of this principle.

Edward Edwards, though greatly assisted by many people (especially by Edwin Abbott, the Headmaster of Marylebone Philological School), was largely self-taught; he was an avid reader and student all his life, and produced a number of scholarly works himself. Antonio Panizzi entered the University of Parma at the age of seventeen, and took a degree in jurisprudence four years later; having fled to London for political reasons, he was eventually appointed to the Chair of Italian Language and Literature at the University of London; and during his lifetime, apart from his great practical achievements as Keeper of Printed Books in the British Museum, he also found time to prepare editions of the works of Boiardo and Dante. Melvil Dewey, from the outset of his life, was constantly studying and reading; and in due course he attended and graduated from Amherst College, his arrangement of the library of which was the foundation of his great classification scheme.

The tenth principle of librarianship is: *A librarian is an educator.*

This principle was most strikingly enunciated in the seventeenth century by John Durie in *The reformed librarie-keeper*. Durie was contemptuous of those librarians who see librarianship only as a means of obtaining 'an easie subsistence', and he expressed the true philosophy thus: 'For if Librarie-keepers did understand themselves in the nature of their work, and would make themselves as they ought to bee, useful in their places in a publick waie; they ought to becom Agents for the advancement of universal Learning'.

Durie's belief in the principle that a librarian is an educator, an Agent for the advancement of universal Learning, was echoed by Henry Evelyn Bliss more than three hundred years later, when he dedicated his work on the organisation of knowledge in libraries to the librarian 'who is organiser and educator'. It was also the main principle which motivated the careers of Edward Edwards, Antonio Panizzi and Melvil Dewey.

Edward Edwards in his *Memoirs of libraries* attempted to define what the duties of librarianship are, and he began by pointing out that as a profession it will never open for an individual a path to wealth or popular fame, and indeed may expose him to social indifference and misconception. Nevertheless: 'By the enlightened and zealous discharge of its functions, a man's work may be made to carry within it the unfailing seeds of many mental harvests, only to be fully gathered in, when he shall have long lain in his grave'.

Edwards lived firmly by his own principle. From his youth onwards, he involved himself in multifarious activities which aimed to promote education generally: for example his early

216

connections with both the Central Society of Education and the Art Union of London. Even during his busy and troubled time as Librarian at Manchester he still lent active support to the Public School Association, which was helping to prepare the way for the Education Act of 1870.

Panizzi's first employment in England after fleeing Italy for political reasons was in teaching, this culminating in his gaining the Chair of Italian Language and Literature at the University of London in 1828. And his philosophy of librarianship during his great years in the British Museum Library was summed up in the evidence he gave before the Select Committee appointed to enquire into its affairs. 'I want a poor student,' he declared, 'to have the same means indulging his learned curiosity, of following his rational pursuits, of consulting the same authorities, of fathoming the most intricate inquiry as the richest man in the kingdom, as far as books go, and I contend that the Government is bound to give him the most liberal and unlimited assistance in this respect.' To the same committee he also observed that the 'most important and most noble purpose' of the British Museum Library was to be 'an establishment for the furtherance of education for study and research'.

Melvil Dewey wrote in his diary at the age of seventeen as follows: 'I have now about fully decided to devote my life to education. I wish to inaugurate a higher education for the masses.' Though he obtained a teaching certificate while still very young, he in the event turned first to librarianship as a way of pursuing his determination to be an educator. One fruit of this was his setting up of the modern world's first library school, at Columbia. Later in his life, he spent eleven very busy years in general educational administration, as Secretary of the New York State Board of Regents, fighting to bring about long overdue reforms in the face of pressures and attacks of every kind. And also in the cause of education he eventually founded the Lake Placid Club, a cooperative vacation-club which Dewey himself styled 'a university in the woods'.

217

The eleventh principle of librarianship is: *A librarian's rôle can only be an important one if it is fully integrated into the prevailing social and political system.*

The earlier principle that libraries are centres of power does not itself make the librarian's rôle an important one. The rôle of the librarian in ancient Egypt was important because it was held in combination with high political rank. The same was true of ancient Babylonia and Assyria, where the librarian of a temple library would also be a priest of high rank, and the librarian of a palace library an important official. The rôle of librarian was, in sum, fully integrated into the prevailing social and political system.

Demetrios of Phaleron, before becoming the first librarian of the Alexandrian Library, had been for a ten-year period of his life the governor of Athens (317-307BC). He was a man of style, power and presence, a highly-placed adviser in the court of Ptolemy Soter. It was Demetrios who suggested to Ptolemy Soter the establishment at Alexandria of both the Museum and the Library. Demetrios's position in court enhanced his rôle as librarian, for the achievements of the Alexandrian Library required political support as well as professional skill.

Libraries and librarians can never afford to be inward-looking. In the nineteenth century, Edward Edwards brought about the provision of free libraries throughout Britain by a lifetime of public crusade and political lobbying. His first triumph was the passing in 1850 of the Public Libraries Act, but he continued to battle on for the provision everywhere, not of 'professional libraries' or of 'tradesmen's libraries' or of 'working men's libraries', but of libraries which would serve every sector of the population, 'attractive to the uneducated and the half-educated' as well as capable of assisting 'the pursuits of the clergyman, the merchant, the politician and the professional scholar'.

Antonio Panizzi was an equally outward-looking and committed individual, seeking just as strenuously to integrate his rôle and that of the British Museum Library into the British

218

social and political system. His life was one long public storm, from his appointment to the Keepership of Printed Books to his retirement as Principal Librarian. He was determined to make the British Museum Library a national library worthy of his adopted country, and he was no less determined to make it available to all.

Melvil Dewey virtually created the profession of librarianship in America, seeing it as a great opportunity for service to society. He preached librarianship as being something which was active, positive, vigorous, and fully integrated socially and politically.

The twelfth principle of librarianship is: *A librarian needs training and/or apprenticeship.*

The librarians of the clay-tablet libraries of Babylonia and Assyria, which existed a thousand years even before Ashurbanipal's Library at Nineveh, bore the title *Nisu-duppi-satri*, 'Man of the written tablets'. These librarians were well-trained. They had to be graduates of the school for scribes, and thoroughly acquainted with the literature or type of records they were to keep. After this initial professional education, they then served an apprenticeship in a library for a number of years, learning several languages at the same time.

The principle that a librarian needs training and/or apprenticeship did not re-emerge in such a full form until the nineteenth century. The landmark then was the establishment by Melvil Dewey of his library school at Columbia in 1887. In the intervening ninety years, library schools have proliferated, the first full-time school in Britain being that set up at University College, London, with the aid of a five-year grant from the Carnegie Trust. The need for professional education has now become fully accepted, along with the realisation that apprenticeship or practical experience is the other essential ingredient in the making of a well-trained librarian.

It is revealing to examine the careers of the great pioneers in the light of this principle. Edward Edwards served his apprenticeship in librarianship at the British Museum Library, as a cataloguer. His professional education—as opposed to actual experience—was a matter he took in hand himself. The publication in 1848 of his *Remarks on the paucity of libraries freely open to the public, in the British Empire; together with a succinct statistical view of the existing provision of Public Libraries in the several states of Europe* revealed his knowledge of what was taking place in libraries generally; but it is his great work, *Memoirs of libraries* (1859), which is the mammoth proof of the breadth of his knowledge of library matters generally.

Antonio Panizzi, even while a boy, was introduced to the world of books by Gaetano Fantuzzi, a former professor of rhetoric, who was in charge of the communal library at Reggio. And while at the University of Parma, he likewise became a friend of Angelo Pezzana, the learned librarian of the Biblioteca Parmense. It may be inferred that it was from these men that Panizzi gained his professional ideals and goals. As for apprenticeship, he of course, like Edward Edwards, began his career as a librarian in the British Museum Library; but unlike Edwards, who in 1851 was appointed Librarian of the Manchester Free Library, Panizzi stayed on at the British Museum Library and transformed it.

Melvil Dewey was self-trained, and self-taught professionally. He served his apprenticeship as college librarian at Amherst. As for professional education, he began as master rather than as student, since it was he who began library school development in America.

The thirteenth principle of librarianship is: *It is a librarian's duty to increase the stock of his library.*

The historian Josephus recorded that Demetrios of Phaleron, the first librarian of the Alexandrian Library, was anxious to collect, if he could, all the books in the inhabited world, and, if he heard of, or saw, any book worthy of study, he would buy it. Indeed, there was a startling degree of ruthlessness in the Alexandrian Library's collection-building policy. Demetrios collected in less than twelve years some 200,000 papyrus rolls. Ptolemy Philadelphus and his successor Ptolemy Euergetes caused all books imported into Egypt by foreigners to be seized, transcribed, the copies delivered to the owners, and the originals deposited in the Library; Euergetes also borrowed the works of Sophocles, Euripides and Aeschylus from the Athenians, and returned only copies. And more perversely, according to Plutarch, when Eumenes II (197-159BC) attempted with his own library at Pergamon to compete in size with the Alexandrian, the Egyptians cut off the supply of papyrus being sent to Pergamon, which in turn led perforce to the development there of a new writing material, parchment (from the Latin *Pergamene*), as a substitute.

Ashurbanipal, too, followed the principle that it is a librarian's duty to increase the stock of his library. He sent agents to every part of his empire, and to foreign lands also, to collect written records of all kinds and on all subjects, until he eventually accumulated a library at Nineveh of some 30,000 clay tablets.

Even in the Middle Ages, when collection-building was at its most difficult, the same principle was followed. Indeed, one of the rules relating to a particular mediaeval library stipulates: 'The first duty of a librarian is to strive, in his time, as far as possible, to increase the library committed to him'.

John Durie, writing in the seventeenth century, stressed the need for a librarian to increase his stock of books and manuscripts even to the extent of suggesting that his performance in this respect should be judged once a year 'by the chief Doctors of each facultie of the Universitie', who should receive 'the Accounts of his Trading, that hee may shew them wherein the stock of Learning hath been increased, for that year's space'. It may be observed, without cynicism, that this is precisely what every librarian in the world still does in his annual report to his committee.

In modern times, every great library is solid proof of the centuries-long adherence of librarians to this principle. The present size of the Library of Congress, with its 64,000,000 items, can be traced back to the efforts of such individuals as its first great librarian, Ainsworth Rand Spofford, who has been described as the Cecil Rhodes of that institution.

221

Spofford in his time built up the Library of Congress, single-mindedly, to a collection of 740,000 volumes. Panizzi performed the same service at the British Museum Library, his aim being to make the Library supreme, not only in Great Britain, but in the world. To do so, he strove successfully for the proper enforcement of the Copyright Act; and he employed active book-agents throughout Europe and the United States.

Even Edward Edwards and Melvil Dewey, who are not commonly regarded as collection-builders, followed the principle that it is a librarian's duty to increase the stock of his library. Edward Edwards, at the time of his dismissal from the Librarianship of Manchester Free Library, had in seven years built up from scratch a collection of some 50,000 volumes. And the libraries of Amherst and Columbia, particularly the latter, grew considerably while under the care of Melvil Dewey.

The fourteenth principle of librarianship is: *A library must be arranged in some kind of order, and a list of its contents provided.*

'Be the collection of Books whatever, were it of fifty thousand Volumes,' wrote Gabriel Naudé in the seventeenth century, 'it would no more merit the name of a Library, than an assembly of thirty thousand men the name of an Army, unless they be martially in their several quarters, under the conduct of their Chiefs and Captains.'

This is a striking formulation of the first part of a principle which has been followed without any deviations right from the beginning of library history. At Edfu, in ancient Egypt, the papyri in the library there were kept in two coffers, works on magic being separated from other works. The clay tablets in the libraries of ancient Babylonia and Assyria were systematically grouped. Ashurbanipal's Library at Nineveh was apparently disposed about the rooms of his palace according to a set plan. The Alexandrian Library was divided into a number of special halls. In the libraries of the early Middle Ages theological books were kept apart from secular books. In early university libraries the books were arranged according to the teaching curriculum. In modern times, formal classifications are the rule.

The second part of the principle, that a list of the contents of a library should be provided, has likewise been unvaryingly maintained for three thousand years. The library at Edfu had a catalogue comprising two registers, the first listing the contents of twelve coffers, the second the contents of the remaining twenty-two. The tens of thousands of clay tablets in the libraries of Babylonia and Assyria were listed and catalogued, as were those in Ashurbanipal's Library. For the Alexandrian Library, Callimachus prepared a classified catalogue, on slips of paper called Penakes; on each slip was written a short title which corresponded exactly with the label on the appropriate papyrus roll. Catalogues of mediaeval libraries were made from the earliest times, and examples survive from the eighth century onwards. Modern times have seen one long unbroken line of catalogue development, from printed catalogues such as that of the Bodleian Library of 1605, down to present-day computer-based systems.

The fifteenth principle of librarianship is: *Since libraries are storehouses of knowledge, they should be arranged according to subject.*

This principle is self-evident, but again the historical support for it endorses its validity. All modern schemes of library classification—Dewey, Universal Decimal Classification, Library of Congress, Bliss—are designed for arrangement by subject. Prior to modern times, arrangement by subject was also the rule, though in less sophisticated form. The Library rooms in Ashurbanipal's palace were each devoted to a particular subject group: one room for tablets relating to history and government, another to those concerning legends and mythology, and so on. Each of the ten halls of the Alexandrian Library was assigned to a separate department of learning. And in mediaeval times, secular works (for example) were arranged according to the *trivium* and *quadrivium*, the former comprising grammar, logic and rhetoric, and the latter arithmetic, geometry, music and astronomy.

The sixteenth principle of librarianship is: *Practical convenience should dictate how subjects are to be grouped in a library.*

Both Ashurbanipal's Library and the Alexandrian Library were arranged for practical convenience rather than according to any philosophical classification of knowledge. This was also true of early modern schemes such as that of Konrad Gesner (1516-1565), whose *Pandectarum sive partitionum universalum* (1548-9) was based on the mediaeval enumeration of studies (the *trivium* and *quadrivium*) already mentioned, and which therefore in a practical fashion followed the order in which the successive studies in a university are pursued. The identical principle lay behind the classification of the Bodleian Library which, when it was first opened in 1602, was divided into four subject groups or Faculties: Theology, Law, Medicine and Arts. And later in the same century, when Gabriel Naudé published his *Bibliothecae Cordesianae catalogus*, he described the classification he used as the most 'practified', since it followed 'the Faculties of Theology, Physick, Jurisprudence, Mathematicks, Humanities and others' in its arrangement.

In recent times the arrangement of libraries has been dominated by two schemes in particular—the Dewey Decimal Classification (with its derivative, the Universal Decimal Classification) and the Library of Congress Classification. The characteristic shared by these schemes is that each is utilitarian. Dewey himself described his system as a series of pigeon-holes into which material might be fitted, and his nine main classes as being in reality nine special classifications. The Library of Congress scheme is built on the same model— a series of special classifications practically conjoined. Schemes which have relied on a philosophical classification of knowledge have not found so wide an adoption, and indeed most—such as that of James Duff Brown—have long since been abandoned.

The seventeenth, and final, principle of librarianship is: *A library must have a subject catalogue.*

This principle is a logical extension of previous principles relating to the fact that a library is a storehouse of knowledge arranged by subject. Again though, library history bears out the logic. The earliest library catalogues were subject catalogues. Callimachus's *Penakes*, as has been seen, took the form of a classified catalogue. Mediaeval catalogues were of short titles arranged by subject. Not until the period 1200-1300, with the appearance of the union list *Tabulae Septem Custodiarum super Bibliam*, was alphabetical arrangement by author introduced.

The eminence of the subject catalogue continued into the age of the printed book, with catalogues such as those of Aldus Manutius and Robert Estienne. Though the author catalogue had established itself by the eighteenth and nineteenth centuries, even in the latter century a Parliamentary Committee of 1849 (which was appointed to enquire into public libraries) concluded: 'So far as they have enquired, it appears to your committee that a catalogue, classified as to subjects, with an alphabetical list of authors, would be best'.

Indeed, the period 1800-1850 in Britain produced a multiplicity of classed catalogues, but the subject arrangements were too often artificial and the order within them not sufficiently systematic. Consequently a reaction against such catalogues followed in the latter half of the century, a reaction which was met by the introduction of the dictionary catalogue. Andrea Crestadoro's Index Catalogue was a crude form of this, but it was Charles Ammi Cutter in America who produced the standard code of rules for the compilation of dictionary catalogues.

The printed dictionary catalogue held sway until the turn of the century, when card catalogues became more common; and in card form since, the majority of libraries in this century have continued to provide a subject catalogue—either classified or alphabetical—to their collections.

Bibliography

BLADES, William: *The enemies of books.* London, Elliot Stock, 1902.

BLISS, Henry Evelyn: *The organization of knowledge in libraries and the subject-approach to books.* 2nd ed, New York, H W Wilson, 1939.

BOSTWICK, Arthur E: *The American public library.* New York, Appleton, 1910.

CLARK, John Willis: *The care of books.* Cambridge, Cambridge UP, 1901.

DURIE, John: *The reformed librarie-keeper.* London, printed by William Dugard, 1650.

EDWARDS, Edward: *Libraries and founders of libraries.* London, Trübner, 1865.

Memoirs of libraries. 2 vols, London, Trübner, 1859.

ESDAILE, Arundell: *National libraries of the world: their history, administration and public services.* 2nd ed, by F J Hill, London, Library Association, 1957.

GOODRUM, Charles A: *The Library of Congress.* New York, Praeger, 1974.

IRWIN, Raymond: *The English library.* London, Allen & Unwin, 1966.

The heritage of the English library. London, Allen & Unwin, 1964.

The origins of the English library. London, Allen & Unwin, 1958.

JOHNSON, Elmer D: *History of libraries in the western world.* 2nd ed, Metuchen, NJ, Scarecrow Press, 1970.

KELLY, Thomas: *A history of public libraries in Great Britain, 1845-1965.* London, Library Association, 1973.

KENYON, Sir Frederick: *Libraries and museums.* London, Benn, 1930.

MILLER, Edward: *Prince of librarians: the life and times of Antonio Panizzi of the British Museum.* London, Deutsch, 1967.

MUNFORD, W A: *Edward Edwards, 1812-1886: portrait of a librarian.* London, Library Association, 1963.

NORRIS, Dorothy May: *A history of cataloguing and cataloguing methods, 1100-1850.* London, Grafton, 1939.

PARSONS, Edward Alexander: *The Alexandrian Library, glory of the Hellenic world: its rise, antiquities, and destructions.* London, Cleaver-Hume Press, 1952.

PINNER, H L: *The world of books in classical antiquity.* Leiden, Sijthoff, 1958.

RIDER, Fremont: *Melvil Dewey.* Chicago, American Library Association, 1944.

The scholar and the future of the research library: a problem and its solution. New York, Hadham Press, 1944.

SAVAGE, Ernest A: *Old English libraries: the making, collection, and use of books during the Middle Ages.* London, Methuen, 1911.

THOMPSON, C Seymour: *Evolution of the American public library, 1653-1876.* Washington, Scarecrow Press, 1952.

THOMPSON, James Westfall: *Ancient libraries.* Berkeley, California UP, 1940.

THORNTON, John L: *The chronology of librarianship.* London, Grafton, 1941.

Index of names

231